LOVE *AND* CHOICE

A Radical Approach to Sex and Relationships

Also by Lucy Fry

Easier Ways to Say I Love You

Run, Ride, Sink or Swim:
A rookie's year in women's triathlon

LOVE
AND
CHOICE

A Radical Approach to Sex and Relationships

LUCY FRY

HODDERstudio

First published in Great Britain in 2022 by Hodder Studio
An Imprint of Hodder & Stoughton
An Hachette UK company

1 3 5 7 9 10 8 6 4 2

A CIP catalogue record for this title is available from the British Library

Trade Paperback ISBN 9781529363593
eBook ISBN 9781529363555
Audio ISBN 9781529363562
Paperback ISBN 9781529363579

Typeset in Garamond Premier Pro by Manipal Technologies Limited

Printed and bound by in Great Britain by Clays Ltd, Elcograf S.p.A.

Hodder & Stoughton policy is to use papers that are natural, renewable and recyclable products and made from wood grown in sustainable forests. The logging and manufacturing processes are expected to conform to the environmental regulations of the country of origin.

Hodder & Stoughton Ltd
Carmelite House
50 Victoria Embankment
London EC4Y 0DZ

www.hodder.co.uk

For anyone who feels they *should* instead of *could*.
I hope this book will bring you choice.
Love *and* choice.

'Instead of looking to a relationship for shelter, we could welcome its power to wake us up in those areas where we are asleep and where we avoid naked, direct contact with life.'

– John Welwood, *Journey of the Heart: The Path of Conscious Love*

A NOTE ON LOVE *AND* CHOICE

Throughout this book I will be making plenty of statements about relationships and therapy as if they are de facto correct. I will be outlining different theories and ideas that I believe are helpful in the development of more conscious, choice-ist relationships and can, in the long run, deepen purpose and meaning in any individual's life. That's fine – we all need a guide sometimes, and in this book, I'll happily be yours – but please keep in mind the biggest truth of all: everything is subjective. I can only offer you my hope, strength and experience through my own professional and personal lens. Over and above all that is this: *you are the greatest expert on yourself.*

Every exercise in these pages is created with the objective of offering you the chance to delve further into the essence of who you are and what you truly want. Change doesn't always happen overnight, no matter how much we want it to. It could take weeks, months or years for you to uncover what's really holding you back and which direction you want to go in. Try, if possible, to enjoy, or at least embrace, the process. Allow yourself to be as loud or quiet as you wish – laugh, cry, shout and/or shake as you journey towards self-awareness, leaving your old, limiting ideas behind and carving out a new freedom for yourself.

With courage and love,
Lucy x

CONTENTS

PROLOGUE

Why Choice?

B and I had been together for nine years, and civilly partnered for seven, when we realised we needed choice.

Our relationship began at boiling point. For the first six months we enjoyed regular sex marathons, erotic-message exchanges and an embarrassing yet regular game of Love Poetry Tennis. Somewhere between six months and a year, however, we began to simmer. We got engaged and kept simmering until we got hitched and began to cool. Our lives were full of love and resentment, dishwasher tablets, home furnishings and family gatherings. Sex became a bimonthly event, often fraught with dejection. There were still glimpses of true erotic connection, but they were all too regularly blighted by mismatched libidos and all-consuming work – and workout – schedules. We supported one another as best we could, both through the everyday difficulties and the big life struggles. We weren't good at carving out time for our relationship; we took holidays sometimes, although one of us usually chose to work at least a little during this sacrosanct time. We drifted away from each other in ways I find very hard to articulate, and which still feel quite painful to think about, but that I know resulted from everyday omissions rather than gaping black holes.

As a therapist, I have heard many clients share similar stories about intimate relationships that started so well, full of possibility and promise, and then slowly (almost imperceptibly) became tense with confusion and frustration. People enter the therapy room wondering where it all went wrong. One common scenario in long-term relationships is that the erotic has been all but swallowed up by the domestic; there is no space left for exploring. Another serious issue is familiarity, which leads people to (often wrongly) assume they know what the other wants. A third, even more prevalent issue is around propriety: the following of a series of entrenched ideas about what is or is not acceptable to seek or want, sexually and/or romantically.

I have watched so many times as clients, friends or acquaintances speak about sex and desire in a secretive, shameful tone (no eye contact, shoulders hunched), admitting that there is something 'else' they sometimes crave – an exploration or an adventure; something they are sure they should not need and daren't ask for.

'Maybe I just shouldn't be in any intimate relationship,' they say.

'It always ends up the same way . . . There's something wrong with me.'

'I think I want the closeness, and the security, of something solid and loving, but then at some point I start to feel suffocated, bored even.'

'Am I perverted? I have these fantasies . . .'

'I think it's me; it's all my fault. It hurts, though, so much; nobody sees.'

'What I really want? Ha-ha, that's funny. What I want is definitely not allowed.'

Not only do I hear these kinds of self-limiting thoughts and feelings often, but I can also empathise. There is something quite insidious – more generally, in human nature perhaps, but also in our society – about the need to self-chastise or pathologise, particularly when we are hurting or unhappy.

Some people try to blame themselves, while others prefer to blame another. Most often, they oscillate between the two, but invariably it is blame that is a central feature of whatever explanation (for these desires) is constructed. In short: judgement wins over curiosity, with a focus on the past, rather than the future.

Sadly, for me, this is familiar – it's something B and I did for years as we tried to find a reason why our relationship felt sticky, ill-fitting even, and why we could not just 'fix it'. What I can see now, with the benefit of hindsight, is that although we talked *a lot,* we actually did not communicate very well, spending long hours discussing our relationship (sex, intimacy, living arrangements, love languages, etc.), but rarely getting to the crux of things. We would continue to circle around entrenched issues that, without the guidance of a professional third party, were unlikely to ever be fully resolved.

For a long time, we did not brave the kind of radical honesty that has the power to slice through even the biggest knots. We rarely spoke about desire with any real courage or conviction, and I, for one, continued to feel quite terrible about it all: my secret fantasies and furtive yearnings for something/someone else. I tried to tell myself that it was just an addictive tendency, that everyone in long-term relationships felt this niggling sense of dis-ease and I just had to 'grow up and put up', as one of my parents used to say. I also assumed this was my issue; that I was awful, selfish, *bad.* But still, it didn't stop the thoughts and images that whizzed in and out of my mind whenever they bloody well wanted, while I exhausted myself failing to banish them. I felt stuck, confused and angry. I knew there was a problem – we needed to change *something* – but I could not see a way out. I was too fearful of losing the person I loved to be completely honest with her, and so I lost myself instead.

I have learnt, both at work and at home, that it is exactly this kind of avoidance of the hard-core truth that is most damaging to relationships. Every time you choose to swerve a difficult conversation, to 'white lie' your way to peace or to deny your deeper needs, you are just racking up issues for the future. Think of it like rot inside a building: you can live with the decay for quite a while without noticing until, one day, it is everywhere; the structural integrity is compromised and the whole thing starts to collapse.

After nine years in a relationship with B, my head was turned by someone new. It wasn't the first time, I'll admit, but this time there was such a charge – so much backed-up frustration and longing in me – that it felt irresistible. I felt a strong compulsion to act and although it was a lot about sex, it also didn't feel *all* about sex. I knew I needed to explore this new connection in the way I had needed to pursue any other meaningful longing in my life. It felt interlinked with vitality and creativity – something inside of me that could not wait any longer to be expressed.

Clearly, I couldn't continue with monogamy, yet I felt scared that my now-deafening desire would split us up. So, I did what so many people in long-term relationships do when they are struggling in a similar way: I cheated.

I lied and deceived my partner; I hardly slept; my appetite halved. I hated myself so much. It was awful and it was energising. It was terrifying and liberating. It was both very stressful and very exciting.

After a month or so, I came clean to B what I had done and was still doing. She was upset – furious even – although not completely bewildered as we had joked (sort of) a couple of times in the recent past about how we both felt attracted to non-monogamy. But when B told me her own secret, that she too had cheated two years ago, I felt my guts descend earthwards. That she had done it at all – that hurt my feelings. But that I had not known about it until now? *That* was a bigger deal. It made me feel angry, and strangely frightened. There was something about not having had access to this crucial information – details about who my partner was and what she wanted – as well as the lies, that felt unfair. It took a few months but eventually I realised that I wished I had known so that I could have decided whether or not to stay. I was almost certain that I would have stayed, but the transparency seemed very important – essential, in fact – to my autonomy within our relationship.

The day of the great revelations, B and I wept a lot, then screamed. We held each other as we slept; we woke up angry yet relieved. That is just what it feels like, I think, when a buried truth is unearthed in relationships. It wasn't pretty, but it was real. Of course, I wish we hadn't cheated on each other. I swear I heard both of our hearts rip when we found out, right down the middle. I wish we had been more honest, earlier, and that neither of us had deceived the other, because it did impact on our trust.

Yet I have never regretted what happened next, nor the way that things unfolded. Over the course of various difficult and emotionally charged conversations, we began to unpack our relationship. I told B that I still loved her, deeply, but also really wanted to continue to pursue my new connection with this other person, A. B expressed a similar desire to explore.

This was a major turning point for us. We had to either build a new kind of relationship, conscious and honest at its core, or walk away from one another completely. We chose to stay, and to transform. The main aspect of our transformation was, initially at least, a relocation, as we shifted the nature of our relationship from (supposedly) monogamous to consciously – some call this 'ethically' – non-monogamous.

The first two years in particular were very challenging and included more tears, anxiety, anger, break-ups and make-ups than I thought humanly possible. This alien land of Conscious Non-Monogamy (CNM for short) was not nearly as habitable, and far more intimidating, than I'd imagined. Yes, it was exciting and inspiring, with beautiful mountain tops and lush, impressive views, but there were also switchback paths, steep drops and a distinct lack of inhabitants. As time went on I realised that I should have brought a map, or at least thought about looking at one *before* I decided to leave the rather more charted land of Monogamy. I had no idea what I was doing here, in CNM, nor did I know my way around some of the villages – Polyamory, Polyfidelity, Swinging, Open Marriage and the very large town called Everything Inbetween.

The other thing that was so difficult was people's reactions to our plight. Granted, I didn't expect a welcoming committee, but nor did I expect the Lifestyle Police. I felt shocked at how many of my friends and family were incredulous and upset with me for choosing to be non-monogamous. Weirder still, they seemed far more comfortable talking about other people's illicit affairs. Some even acknowledged that they found it easier to see a partner being actively deceived by another partner than to watch an entire partnership transform itself, consensually, into something quite new.

This made sense because for most people, me included, monogamy isn't just a sexual or romantic choice, but an entire system upon which love and relationships are built. For those who think of monogamy as the default position, any deviance from it is potentially uncomfortable. But recognising that conscious non-monogamy frightens lots of people does not mean you should not, or cannot, go there yourself. I'd just advise that if you want to live/holiday/take a sabbatical in the land of CNM, be cautious about who you tell, and who you go to for support. Sometimes it is those who you think will be most mentally flexible who shut the door right in your face, whereas those you thought were super-conventional have minds with lots of space to wander.

With hindsight, I can see that the way we presented it did not help. Neither me nor B nor my newer partner, A, had any idea how best to approach CNM. We lived in a state of perpetual drama and confusion, and this must have come across clearly when we spoke about it. I suspect people listening thought, *This is mad – these guys are doing all this weird stuff and they aren't even happy!* We were open-minded, yes, but also uneducated, unprepared and full of the typical angst and insecurities that come hand in hand with being human. For every useful mistake we made, there was another that caused unnecessary suffering. Mostly they were the result of one of us either not having thought things through or not having established appropriate boundaries.

We tried, of course, to self-educate. We listened to podcasts and read books on non-monogamy and polyamory, attended some relevant events and talks, and even joined forums (remember those?) online. The material presumed non-monogamy was to be constant, and I was unconvinced I wanted it long term. Firstly, we had relocated to Non-Monogamy™ in a crazy rush after recognising (too late) that Monogamy™ had become uninhabitable, which felt a bit like learning how to fix a tyre only *after* getting a puncture. All I was certain of was that 'default' monogamy was no longer working for me and that I wanted more choice about what constituted fidelity. But did that mean I had to choose non-monogamy, and be non-monogamous forever? I yearned to read something about relationships that gave me permission to wonder and imagine who I was, and what I wanted, without asking me to do anything specific or forcing me to adhere to any particular label.

As time went on, I kept searching for that book. I was also listening to more and more people, both friends and clients, share honestly their relationship struggles; how they felt they had no choice and how they had to fit 'the blueprint' of a monogamous, long-term pairing that included certain hallmarks, such as cohabiting, family-making and shared finances. I began to wonder if, rather than waiting for someone else to produce the book that I was looking for – the book I felt so many people needed – I ought to write it myself.

INTRODUCTION

The Matter of Choice

What, in your relationships, have you chosen? What would you choose if you felt able?

Most of us are brought up with a blueprint – an outline or even a plan – for our most important and intimate relationships. It can be more or less explicit, sent via parents, grandparents, teachers, the media, books, television or even the government's tax policies, but the message we receive is simple:

> *The (gold) standard for a romantic relationship is one that is heterosexual, between two people, and monogamous.*

But why is that the standard, and is it working for you, really? Some people recognise their uniqueness early on and are forced to question and/or defy this blueprint. For example: if they are attracted to the same sex (or both sexes, lots of sex or just no sex at all . . .), if their gender identity doesn't match their birth assignment or their desires are forbidden by their religion. Many people go for decades without wondering about whether 'the norm' really works for them, becoming entrenched in relationship ideals and systems that may no longer make so much sense.

The brave among them start to wonder:

> *What do I really want from a romantic relationship? Who am I really? Who might I be?*

In both my last few years spent working as a therapist and over a decade of writing professionally about health, wellbeing and relationships, I have spent much time exploring the human psyche and its shadows. I have been astonished by the prevalence of the relationship blueprint – those limiting beliefs about who we should be and how we should behave when it comes to sex, romance, intimacy and love – and also felt dismayed by its power.

I have watched people become unhappy and unwell trying to adhere to supposed rules that no longer serve them. Yet I have also watched some of those same people – myself included – dig deep to free themselves. I know which one I'd recommend.

So, how do we find freedom in relationships, both with others and with ourselves? I think it begins with a sense of choice, by which I mean believing in and respecting the idea that one has some agency in one's life and the direction that it takes. I believe that when we respect choice, notice choice, enact choice and live in line with choice, we can access a deep and important sense of freedom, and live more responsible, conscious lives.

I know that might sound idealistic, but, far from being about lofty, intellectual principles, this requires one to have one's feet firmly on the ground and get stuck into the very real, everyday stuff of being a body as well as a mind. Yet although I would argue that conscious choice is not elitist, I can hardly argue that it is even-handed. No sensible person would suggest that life, with all its inequalities and accidents, offers each individual access to the same number or types of choices. What I do trust, however, is that there is always some level of choice available to everyone. Even when a situation feels challenging, we have a choice about what perspective to take or who we share our worries with.

Perhaps you are one of those people who has decided they don't have options: this is your lot, and that is that. Maybe you think that this is because of your circumstances, rather than your mindset. You might think, for example, that parents are in a different camp from all other adults; they can't afford the luxury of such broad choices because what they choose impacts on their children. That may be right, but choice remains available, despite the fact that everyone's personal circumstances differ. Having dependants, or challenging circumstances, does not mean you have no choice. What about other kinds of carers? Those who live with disability? With poverty? Or with major mental health issues? If I had a ten-pound note for every time someone had said to me, *You don't understand, it's different for me because of*. . . I think I could finally visit the Arctic. Of course, each of these people are right. We are all different, yes. But there is *always* more room for choice.

Who Is This Book For?

The simplest answer is: *almost* everyone. The ideas within these pages can be considered, questioned and (at least in part) adopted by anybody, regardless of age, sex, ethnicity, gender identity, sexuality, political leanings or relationship status. This book is just as much about inquiring into your unique relational needs and wants as it is about telling stories from other walks of life or offering suggestions about relationship building. It is about opening yourself to new possibilities. What I hope is that by the end of this book you'll be free to change or stay the same – consciously.

Much of this book's focus is the practice of reclaiming *choice* amid the confines of the blueprint – *heterosexual, between two people, and monogamous.* Almost all of us can benefit from introducing more conscious choice into our lives, and not just around relationships, but also things like health, money, work and lifestyle. Some people will read this book and immediately make necessary positive changes in various aspects of their lives, others may merely experience the kind of intellectual and emotional spaciousness that can be achieved by even a slight switch in perspective. Both types of change are valid.

This book is written as much for married or long-term couples who have zero intention of moving away from monogamy as it is for those who are reaching a crossroads in their relationship and are thinking about where to go next. It is for anybody who is feeling stuck, or is in a transitional phase, from those entering or leaving a relationship, having children or watching those children leave home, to those who are going through the menopause (or manopause – yes, that's a real thing, when men experience a decrease in testosterone). It is as relevant to fiercely committed polyamorists, who would never dream of dating just one person, as it is to committed singletons, who can't imagine sharing their physical, emotional or mental space at all. I also hope that, for those who are struggling with but committed to non-monogamy, this book will provide inspiration, hope and support.

There are only two types of people that this book may not touch, or positively impact, and they are mostly atypical. They are either those early adopters who are already asking choice-focused questions in all aspects of their lives or, at the other end of the spectrum, those who question nothing and are mentally unable to adopt any other kind of perspective, even for a moment.

That's not you, though. Is it?

Love and *Choice* – What to Expect

Love and *Choice is:*

- A guide to help you think differently about relationships; become less guarded and more honest with yourself and your partner(s); delve deeper into your physical and emotional desires; create more authentic connections without entirely sacrificing your sense of identity or passion.
- A collection of stories from those who have moved away from the typical relationship or lifestyle blueprint and made conscious choices to do things in a more radical way.
- A starting point from which to explore a few key therapeutic ideas or ways of thinking that could enhance your relationships, big time. These include considering how you make and break relationships

(what patterns you have) and what parts of yourself you might have pushed to the very edges of your consciousness and how that might be hindering you.
- A book that builds upon the existing small-yet-excellent group of titles that cover ways of thinking about, developing or enjoying relationships that don't fit neatly into the monogamous paradigm.

Love and *Choice is not:*

- A substitute to individual or couples' psychotherapy.
- An attempt to persuade its readers or their lovers/spouses/friends/family that a non-monogamous life is in any way better than a monogamous life, or vice-versa. Or that these are the only two possibilities. The relative merit of any option is always subjective and no one choice must be made forever.
- A straightforward guide on 'how to open up your relationship'. It doesn't contain instructions and is not another 'How to' guide to non-monogamy or any other specific kind of relationship. Rather, it helps you to write, and re-write, your own guide – one that works for where you are *now*.
- Just about sex. This book does include frequent references to sex, sexual practices and sexuality, yes, but it is no more about sex than it is about marriage or about love. Rather, it is focused primarily on how to live a life full of choice – a life that allows one to change, grow and evolve – both in relation to other people and oneself.

How to Use This Book

I hope that the process of working through this book will help you create nourishing, communicative and truly fulfilling relationships and/or improve on those you have. Certainly, it aims to help you develop a greater awareness of what you really want and the fact that this might change.

Personally, I love scribbling all over books, but if you fancy using a separate notebook, particularly for the Inquiry sections near the end of each chapter, that's a good idea. Wherever you do it, just make some marks – words, sentences, images or angry blobs – when and how you feel like it. It is too easy, with a book like this, to have an important insight and then forget it or not return to mull it over. Yet it is in writing down an insight, and in going back to it later for some further thought, that the real magic happens.

Don't scrimp, is what I'm saying. It is important to be committed to the sometimes-rocky process of self-inquiry. Often what we uncover, in terms of our truer longings or desires in life, love and relationships, are not the most convenient or straightforward. It is crucial, therefore, to pursue choice with a kind of gentle audacity, peering boldly over the cliff and assessing the terrain before you take a giant leap.

In therapy, we talk about making a 'safe container'. It differs from client to client, but in general it does include that the therapy space (not just the physical space, but also the constructs around the therapy, like time boundaries and means of communication between sessions) remains consistent and appropriate. Since this book is – in part, at least – a therapeutic adventure, it feels important to re-create some form of that safety by requesting that you do things in the order they are set down and take brain (and heart) breaks where necessary.

This process can, and will, get tricky. Just like anything that is worth doing. This is something I had to remind myself of regularly in the writing of this book, because even though it was an opportunity I had sought out – one that aligned with my passion, values and purpose – still, it frequently felt overwhelming or exhausting. I really believe, however, that just because something is testing, that does not necessarily mean it is wrong. As I learnt in my years of features journalism, which included many interviews with athletes, our muscles only grow when they are ripped. It is the process of breaking down the tiny fibres that provides the stimulus for adaptation. The muscle analogy is one of the best I can think of to describe the process of developing emotional resilience and self-knowledge. Most types of ongoing therapeutic self-inquiry mirror an athlete's journey: you cannot meet aspirations without experiencing some discomfort or even pain. The sooner you accept this, the easier it will be. Too much intensity, however – too much too fast – leads to injury. As the German writer Johann Wolfgang von Goethe said: 'Do not hurry; do not rest.' It is one thing to push yourself to the edges (or out) of your comfort zone and another to push yourself to breaking point.

How This Book Is Organised

- Chapters One to Four are focused around introducing the idea of conscious choice and identifying ways it might have shown up in, or been hidden from, your life, particularly around relationships. Since recognising that you are on autopilot is the precursor to switching back to manual, we will also take a look at the radical alternatives to the most common relationship structures.
- Chapters Five to Eight cover how to identify the beliefs that have blocked your choices in the past, and how to unpick those entrenched 'life scripts'. As you begin to move beyond these limitations, you can start to be more present and explore the choices that fit, and work for, *you*.
- Chapters Nine and Ten cover choice in action, encouraging you to approach your relational situations in a way that is true to your present whole self. The stories will offer you different relationship maps with options of where to travel. As you explore, I will point out minefields, viewpoints, peaks, troughs or rugged terrain along the way. I will touch on boundaries and transitions as well as commitment and

promises, and also how to work more choice into not just a relationship structure, but your whole life.

- Each chapter will look at different aspects of your life – areas such as sexuality, intimacy or fidelity – where you may have fallen into, rather than chosen, certain beliefs about what you want, or what is right, in relationships. And the stories in each chapter will tackle its themes, portraying different approaches to the norm, their challenges and outcomes, with a summary and opportunities for suggested tasks to help you practise awareness.

A Note on the Stories in This Book

In the researching and writing of this book I have spoken to many people on the topics of relationships. Some of these conversations have been used to form the stories within this book, but all of them have helped me to understand and express the central idea of conscious choice.

Some of the stories include real names; others (marked with *) use pseudonyms. I have been inspired by the honesty and openness from those I have talked to and am deeply grateful to all who have trusted me enough to share their stories. For some, however, being so 'out' is not straightforward. In these cases, not just names but also certain obvious biographical details have been changed.

The interviews that form the backbone of these stories were done over the internet, phone and in person. Video calls included those with Alex*, who was just two miles away at the time (in one lockdown during COVID-19), Dmitri* and Rebecca. I made a series of transatlantic video calls to Cody, Maggie and Janie, interviewing each of them individually at first and then, afterwards, as a witty, triangle-shaped unit all nudged up close to see the screen. Emails were exchanged with Hannah, who I also spoke to on the phone, me in wintry London and her in Santiago, with cathedral bells tolling in the background. Emails and phone calls were exchanged with my friend Elaine, in sunny Seville, and I spoke over the phone to Cath* in rural Cornwall. I took long walks with Anita and Dominic*, drank coffee across the table from Sandy* and Jon* and shared meals with Vix and Cassie*. I enjoyed each of these conversations so much, and learnt a great deal in the process.

CHAPTER 1

CONSCIOUS CHOICE – THE CONCEPT

'Happier Even After' – *Anita's Story (i)*

'I had no idea that I might want other options, or that anybody would . . .'

Anita was in her mid-thirties, living in leafy Kent with her husband and two young children, when she hit her first life crisis.

She had done everything society begged of her, and most of it in the right order. Anita was a straight-A student and the first in her family to attend university, where she studied hard and got an excellent degree. After this, she quickly landed a job in sales and moved to London. It was not so much that she had sat down, thought about it and decided that she wanted to live in the capital, but more that her friends were doing it and, well, wasn't that just what everybody did at this stage?

Her twenties went as expected, as Anita focused on climbing the career ladder, dieting and looking good. By the time she was twenty-six she was team leader and, soon after, chairing conferences. Hobbies? Just drinking, really. In her downtime, Anita partied. It was the early noughties, and Anita's world was awash with dry white wine, cocaine and indistinguishable restaurant chains that served more beer than they did brioche.

'With hindsight, I can see that there was this big disconnect between my mind and my body; my conscious and my unconscious,' says a now-forty-six-year-old Anita. 'I had internalised the supposed set of rules about how to live my life to such a great extent that I could not decipher any other options.'

Is that the paradox of unconsciousness? That one can't see what one can't see? Anita's was not a trajectory she had actively chosen – more a set of aspirations that she had absorbed, growing up in 1980s East Anglia in a home where mainstream tabloid media was consumed without question and standing out was not encouraged. Her father, who had joined the RAF aged seventeen, worked shifts and was often absent for Easter, Christmas, birthdays. His job also meant that the family moved around, so Anita changed schools constantly, which she hated. So much so, in fact, that when she was bullied at school in her teens, she chose being bullied over changing schools once again. Anita buried herself in work, and also reading and television. It wasn't until she arrived in London that something changed. The rules seemed different: being quiet and sensible wasn't normal here. Now, it seemed, people liked savvy. It was a good thing to be social. It was attractive to be flirty. It was enviable to be thin and it was imperative to drink.

'I realised then that I had some sexual capital. I was attractive, thin, bouncy and enthusiastic. I spent my time dashing around the city in tight clothes and renting a flat, solo, in Central London holding down a well-paid job. I thought that I was happy. Or, at least, I assumed I must be, given all I was doing.'

From the outside she looked successful; she was ticking the right boxes. Never mind the fact that Anita was often so drunk on a night out that she could not unlock her own front door. Or that bringing strangers home with her when wasted felt safer than getting into a minicab alone and annihilated. She never questioned her behaviour. This kind of excess was just normalised: the idea of one's twenties was to *have fun,* which meant never taking things too seriously. Her relationships, too, were superficial – more functional than fulfilling, often with a poor sexual and/or emotional connection. They never included any conflict either, something that she would only understand years later could be an important part of a healthy, vibrant relationship.

Aged twenty-eight, Anita met Marc at a singles' party in Central London. Both wore green lights across their tops, the party's designated sign for those who were looking for a relationship. Tall and attractive, Marc was five years older, ran his own business, owned both his own home and a very snazzy sports car. These were the kinds of things that 'blueprint Anita' was taught to look for, that signalled *marriage material.* But was Anita ready for marriage? It was not a question she asked herself. She merely felt the pressure to do it, bombarded by media messages about how heterosexual women who wanted a family had to 'catch' a man before hitting thirty.

Well, 'catch' her man she did, and very quickly too. The trajectory of Anita and Marc's relationship followed the blueprint to a T. They met and exchanged numbers; a few days later they had a phone call and then went on a date. From there, a cinema date, before a third, which included sex, sleepover, breakfast. After that they went away for a weekend to attend a friend's wedding in the countryside, where they stayed at a quaint B&B with squeaky bedsprings and old pine furniture. Next up was *meet the parents.* They were engaged within six months, and from there it was like a checklist:

- Engagement party (drunken)
- Wedding planning (stressful)
- Moving in together (in London)
- Wedding (expensive, gorgeous, drunken)
- Honeymoon (three weeks, South Africa)
- Buying family home (outside London)
- Pregnancy; first baby (boy)
- Pregnancy; second baby (girl)
- Smile. Survive. Smile.
- Happy. Ever. After?

The Blueprint – A Starting Point

The thing that comes through so clearly in Anita's story is the way that a set of expectations can unconsciously govern a person's life. It really *is* possible to take big, life-changing decisions without much awareness. When I think back to my engagement, at twenty-seven, and my ensuing civil partnership a year later, I see that I just had no other perspective. As I walked down the aisle, I was both there and *not* there. Just like Anita, I was propelled to *take the next right step* towards the bigger picture. I cannot truly say that getting hitched was what I wanted. Nor can I say I didn't want it. But I was in love and so . . . of course.

Of course? I did not stop to ask, *But why?* This is the insidious mastery of the blueprint – that it can go so undetected. But what, exactly, is a blueprint? It's defined as a plan from which other drawings can be copied or a real-life structure built. In the context of relationships, I use blueprint to refer to any of the more automatic or pre-programmed ways of loving and living. Blueprints differ across cultures and countries, yet each one reflects the dominant way of the so-called majority and contains the inherent assumption that the dominant way is the right way. A blueprint can change over time too. Centuries ago, in British society, for example, marriage was a strategic move, primarily motivated by status. To marry purely for love was either radical or foolish, whereas nowadays it is regarded as the most honourable, normal reason.

When I use the word blueprint in this book I am, more than anything, referring to something that is followed or inherited, rather than designed and chosen. Sometimes we are actively told that our lives would be better if we did things a certain way. Or the messages are more implicit, floating into our minds via background imagery or what we absorb from the media. Often, too, a blueprint is re-established by virtue of what is omitted from our purview; the narratives that aren't told and the lifestyles that are silenced.

It is almost strange, considering there are so many examples of shifting or different blueprints, that we are so wedded to the notion at all. In the white capitalist world of suburban Southwest London where I grew up, it was clear to me from a young age what the relationship blueprint was. I was to aspire to thinness and femininity, and to express palatable emotions like happiness. I was to keep my sexuality private and to be only mildly opinionated. I should marry a man and have babies. I should be a faithful and loving mother. Cohabit. I was also meant to have a stellar career in something straightforwardly professional, earn money, pay taxes, buy *stuff*.

Suffice it to say I didn't make it. Even if I hadn't been queer, I think I would have struggled to hit those marks. Our society is more inclusive than it was when I was growing up, yet the general expectation around relationships still seems to be that they will include at least one of the following: heterosexuality; two people only; monogamy; marriage or civil partnership; cohabiting; an aspiration to be together long term; children or an aspiration to have them. To be in a relationship that clearly does not include one of these aspects, such as choosing to be married but not live together, or to live together with entirely separate finances, is treated as *odd*. Or, even worse, with suspicion.

Moving Away From the Blueprint

If a blueprint is the master design from which others are copied, then its opposite is nothing at all – to begin with a blank slate. However appealing (or terrifying) this may sound, you can place the blank page on top of the blueprint, choose which lines to trace over, if any, and create your own picture. This is what I hope to offer with this book – the chance to identify your inherited blueprint and the confidence to trace over it with something more bespoke.

To be consciously choosing something, you have to at first know you have a choice.

Take a bird, or a mouse, spider, grasshopper, ant – anything small enough to sit on a human hand. That creature is sitting inside your open palm. Why does it stay? Because it could leave at any point. But the moment the palm becomes a cage, it has no other choice but to stay. Remaining in the cage may be safer – simpler, even – but it is also just a prison. For most of us the biggest cage is, of course, our minds. Yes, you can stay in the cage and have choice, but only when the door is open. Once that door is shut, choice disappears. The trick is to learn how to unlock it yourself.

Do you want to be free to inhabit the person you are right now?

Not the one you were back then?

Not the one you *should* become?

Sometimes the answer is a loud *yes.* Sometimes it is quieter, and hard to hear. Sometimes, as with young Anita, there is just an absence of response because the question itself is out of shot, unavailable to her conscious mind. In this case, we are not yet aware that we are holding onto entrenched ideas that may no longer serve us. Until something starts to itch. We may not even know why; we just aren't happy with the status quo. Something is wrong. Something is brewing. It is often at this point that people seek therapy. *I just don't know where joy went,* they might say, or, *Why am I feeling so stuck? I know I want to quit my job but can't quite do it. I hate my spouse but can't quite leave. Why can't I do it?* They ask: *Why, when I know full well that it's not working, can't I make the change I want to make?*

I like to think of my younger self as a sleepwalker. There I was, living my life as a Monogamous Heterosexual™ until the moment I woke up. Living awake is both fantastic and unnerving because, yes, choice can be scary. It is normal to crave and fear freedom simultaneously, to long for both security and adventure. It is often this supposed conflict in desires, and the perceived impossibility of getting both those needs met simultaneously, that leads people to cheat. Conscious relationship building is about learning to accept and embrace this natural inner conflict and using it as fuel for growth and a means to connect more deeply with others. What's more, there are responsible, loving adults out there who do not believe that we must choose between the familiar and the new, but that we can rather negotiate a way to enjoy both.

Please note that loving freedom isn't the same as anarchy, lovelessness or commitment phobia. This is about ensuring you don't just live in one small room, with all the doors shut, when there's a whole house to explore. If you want to stay in one room, I get it (sometimes I crave small, cosy spaces too), but if you are remaining in there because you didn't realise there were other rooms or floors, then, well, we have a problem.

Conscious choice is more about developing self-governance than trying to control life – yours or anyone else's. As one of the best-known Stoic philosophers, Epictetus, said: 'Make the best use of what's in your power and take the rest as it happens.' He was firm in his insistence that wherever we find ourselves, we can maintain our freedom of choice.* Despite living two thousand years ago, Epictetus really did know a thing or two about this subject, having been born a slave and living with major health issues.

Living in a 'choice-ist' way can be both exhilarating and demanding. Not following a set structure or any pre-established relationship 'rules' can be difficult to say the least. I will never forget the confusion of my first foray into conscious non-monogamy, how exhausting it felt to question what I thought I knew about relationships and their supposed rules. By this stage I was in my mid-thirties, making conscious choices in my work, tenacious in my pursuit of a career as an author and freelance journalist and in a same-sex relationship. This latest identity shift, however, was a

* Epictetus, *Discourses,* 2.6.25. 'A podium and a prison is each a place, one high and another low, but in either place your freedom of choice can be maintained if you so wish.'

whole new level of mind-bending, shaking those around me in a way that my being a queer woman did not. In truth, it shook me more, too, since I was now moving away from the entire mainstream system of relationships.

Perhaps understandably, I felt split between the past and the future. First, there was the old me who wanted to keep on moving with the masses, searching for The One, who would offer me 360 degrees of romantic and sexual satisfaction. Then there was the new me who now believed, deep-down, that such a feat was hardly possible, let alone desirable. I knew I had to learn to stop seeking satisfaction from any other human – expecting anyone to complete or fix me – and that I needed different things from different people. Agreeing to 'together forever' at any age seemed like madness. If a relationship lasted thirty years that was one thing, but promising to stick to any preordained plan that left little room for change and considered that relationship a total failure if it ended? It felt like a commitment to stagnation rather to my own and my lover's (or lovers') growth.

Living a choice-ist life does not actually require you to do anything other than engage in choice with an active mind. Sometimes it is more about mindset than anything else. At other times, it requires action. It is rarely about insisting upon one specific outcome, though – needing to control things to this degree will only shoot you forwards to insanity, rather than gently nudge you towards freedom.

Choice can be incorporated into all aspects of relationships, from sleeping arrangements to housework, to exclusivity or holiday plans. It is primarily for those who wish to maximise their fulfilment on this earth without also creating chaos and destruction. I'll be honest with you: it's not easy. Transformation, I'm afraid, requires shattering and rebuilding ideas that are held dear. There may be someone out there who has evolved, both deeply and for the long term, without any pain, but I have yet to meet them.

The status quo, however unfulfilling, can be very tough to shift, particularly when it's foundational to identity and one's place in the world.

Especially when learnt young. So much of my work with clients is, on one level, dissolving restrictive core beliefs and rewriting life scripts in order to free that person to be more of their true self. Having the freedom to unshackle ourselves from those old roles, to change our minds about who we are and what we want, is the absolute essence of conscious living.

Why I Love Being "Choice-ist"

If there is a common denominator in all shapes and sizes of conscious relationship building, it is the importance of acknowledging *choice.* I like to call this being 'choice-ist'. If I had to sum up what choice-ism offers in the fewest words possible, I would say that it is about turning *should* into *could.* When I have a choice-ist mindset, I own the choices I make. I take responsibility for the part I have played in any fallout my choice(s) may cause. But I don't take responsibility for others' choices. Nor do I pick up their emotional baggage and start carrying it around with me – no way. I've got my own to haul around. Turns out, that's heavy enough.

More than anything, becoming choice-ist is about deciding that whatever your heart truly longs for actually matters, that it is okay to value your desires. It is also about understanding that the way you go about achieving those desires also matters; how we behave and talk has an impact on those around us. Choice-ism is not about the belief that every human being deserves to get everything they want, anytime, anywhere, but about surrendering to the beautiful and challenging process of self-inquiry, to know yourself more fully and make more mindful, truthful choices. In making these conscious choices, we are less likely to blame others for our frustrations because we are living lives with eyes wide open. We are no longer sleepwalking.

In his book *Missing Out: In Praise of the Unlived Life,* psychoanalyst and writer Adam Phillips suggests that every time you feel you are missing out on something and do not pursue it, you are, by default, choosing what you already have. Maintaining the status quo, therefore, is a valid choice in itself. I really like this idea because a) it encourages us to welcome our daydreams and fantasies as a way of ascertaining what we really want and b) it requires us to take pride in continuing with something, as much as we might for opting for something else.

Phillips calls this *choosing by exclusion*. Another way of putting this is that when we live a choice-ist life we get to swap FOMO – 'fear of missing out' – for JOMO – 'joy of missing out'. I know it sounds strange to talk about missing out in the same sentence as joy, but in acknowledging the *choice* to 'miss out' on one option for another, we become creators rather than victims. And that, I think, is joyful.

This (JOMO) only works when the choice is conscious. When we make a choice in full knowledge that there was another path we could have taken, we can experience freedom at greater depths. This comes with responsibility, of course – true freedom always does – but it allows us to own more of our lives.

Here is a simple example, from me, in relation to my writing work: some days writing is wonderful. On others, it is tricky. Every writer in the world will tell you that there are days when the words don't flow. Days when the whole process feels more like peeling chewing gum off fabric. It can take an hour to write four lines. Another hour to delete two. I wonder: *Why am I doing this when I could be in the pub? I could be sleeping, or at the beach.*

The crucial words here are *I could.* So long as the word is *could*, then I am making a choice. When those chewing gum days arrive, rather than complaining, I remind myself of the choice I made to prioritise my writing. Reiterating that does not always take away the struggle, but it does reduce the self-pity (which, along with perfectionism, is the enemy of creativity). When I remember that *I am choosing* to write this book, I am in a JOMO state of mind.

What about more serious issues? Like people who long to have children but can't? Or those who experience systemic racism? Or whose countries are at war? Clearly, they are not choosing their predicament. Yet one's reaction remains a choice. Austrian neurologist and psychiatrist Viktor Frankl put forward a very compelling argument for the all-pervasive nature of choice in his book *Man's Search for Meaning*. Here, he describes the horrific experiences he encountered as a prisoner at a concentration camp in the Second World War. Despite the barbaric conditions and the murder of many of his fellow inmates, Frankl still believed that 'every day, every hour, offered [one] the opportunity to make a decision, a decision which determined whether you would or would not submit to those powers which threatened to rob you of your very self, your inner freedom . . .'*

Frankl insisted that there is always, at least, one choice: the choice to embrace, or not, one's spiritual freedom. In the concentration camp this was the one thing, often the only thing, that could not be taken away from him, whatever was happening.

'Happier Even After' – *Anita's Story (ii)*

Despite following the recommended blueprint, and having everything she was meant to want, thirty-eight-year-old Anita felt increasingly unfulfilled. She spent her days at home with two young children and Marc was working twelve-hour days, five days a week. When they were together, there wasn't much affection or sexual chemistry. No matter how much she loved her children, life was lonely and monotonous; she was still re-establishing herself socially outside London and constantly exhausted from the demands of parenthood.

Anita found herself anaesthetising with alcohol once again. This was different from the wild, nonsensical drinking of her twenties. Now she

* Frankl, V. *Man's Search for Meaning* (Rider, 2004), p.75.

was drinking daily and alone, from the moment her children hit their beds. After one particularly vicious two-day hangover, some of which was spent lurching in the audience of her son's nursery nativity show, Anita finally decided to get help. Thankfully, she managed to quit drinking, and things got better for a year or two. But where alcohol had been, an emptiness now screamed back. There was something more Anita needed. Something that would not go away.

'I remember that first day that both children were at school all day. I had been feeling so trapped and bored. I dropped them [off] and drove straight to the station car park, ran across to get the train and went to London, to a gallery. I loved it so, so much. I'll never forget quite how it felt to feed my brain and breathe in culture.'

After making many day trips like this one, Anita became interested in music. She began going to gigs where she met new, fun people with whom she chatted, danced, flirted. Her libido, dimmed in recent years, began to flicker and reignite. She found herself actively pursuing validation from the men she met, often omitting that she was married. She told herself that she was merely reclaiming a sense of autonomy that she had lost as a mother to infants. She figured that, this way, nothing needed to change at home. But this freedom was short-lived; it soon felt less like the perfect combination and more like she was splitting herself in two.

'I knew I couldn't carry on this way, being one person when I was out and another one at home. I'd heard about open relationships and read a seminal book called *Rewriting the Rules* by M-J Barker, which I gave to Marc to read. He was open-minded and immediately got it. I think he understood, intellectually at least, the benefits of conscious non-monogamy and how it might help with managing the challenges of a long-term relationship.'

The couple tried non-monogamy for about a year, during which time Anita explored *a lot,* both mentally and sexually. Here she was, having multiple connections with different people *and* maintaining her family life at home. A balance she previously thought impossible, selfish even.

This was the best of both worlds, surely? Could Anita literally have her cake *and* eat it?

Yes, was the answer, but also, no. The problem was that Anita had become so hungry for freedom that she gorged on it, sometimes at the expense of both her safety and wellbeing. Her curiosity, having been repressed for so long, became her master, as she exposed herself to excessively intense and overwhelming situations with people who were not on the same wavelength.

'My dominant memories are negative. I was interested in exploring my kinkier side but had no idea how to do that with some degree of self-care,' she confesses. 'Most people I met wanted to go straight to the really hardcore stuff. An assumption was made that it was okay to go straight from *Hello, nice to meet* you to *Here you are in chains, wearing a mask*. I didn't know how to negotiate my boundaries, because I was moving too fast and hadn't learnt how to say no.'

Back in the marital bed, however, things weren't going well either. It was not so much the 'opening up' of Anita and Marc's relationship that was the issue, but more the pre-existing problems that had been left unchecked. The couple still weren't communicating well, with passive aggression and unspoken resentment a common feature. Offering one another sexual freedom, it seemed, had only papered over the cracks.

After six months, Anita met Andrea, a handsome, warm Italian with a strong intellect and charisma. This time the connection wasn't just sexual; they loved each other's company and enjoyed talking about the philosophies behind conscious non-monogamy as well as actively practising it. They had an understanding from the get-go and could empathise with each other's predicament. Andrea had experienced his own struggles harbouring desires to sleep with other people. After a brutally honest conversation, Andrea and his then-partner had tried to open up their relationship. But it quickly emerged that Andrea's girlfriend had not so much embraced their new set-up but merely *permitted* it, asking him to keep it to himself even though he preferred transparency. In this way, he was given an ultimatum – to live a double life or leave. Andrea found this too distressing and the relationship broke down. He was devastated – something which many of his friends could not square up with the fact that he was now keen on Anita. Could he really feel heartbroken about one woman *and* still be falling for another? Yes, was his answer. Yes. Yes. *Yes.*

It was not just the loss of his girlfriend either: at this time, Andrea's mother was also fast disappearing thanks to a vicious, deadly cancer. Anita's father died almost simultaneously after a long and painful battle with lung disease. She says: 'Losing a parent at the same time, a parent with whom we had complex relationships, brought [us] much closer. I remember the Christmas just before that. My dad was dying and my mum was having a mental breakdown and had ignored a lump in her breast for a year. My relationship with Marc was on its knees. I sat in a grim, English holiday resort frantically texting Andrea with my husband next to me, reading.'

It was the following summer that Anita knew her marriage was over. Their family went on a holiday that proved to be cataclysmic. The couple (who had never argued) had a screaming row and slept separately throughout. They could barely look at one another. It was almost their tenth wedding anniversary and instead of a renewal of vows, they decided to break up.

'We lived together, in separate rooms, for another year after that, to ease the transition. We wanted to make our separation the envy of all our friends, but it was a lot more difficult than I ever thought it would be – making changes, separating from my children's father and getting away from that normative set-up we had,' Anita explained. 'But I also knew that it was absolutely the right thing for me, not in a self-serving way but in a deep, instinctive way. I knew it was vital for both me and the kids, even though it led to an objective decrease in my living circumstances, and it took a few years for my relationship with my children to really heal.'

Meanwhile, Anita and Andrea continued to be in a loving, non-monogamous relationship. Unlike previous relationships, this did not follow any linear trajectory or blueprint. They felt extremely lucky to have found, in each other, someone who understood just how central that 'openness' was to their principles and sense of self. They promised, above all else, to support each other in pursuing freedom in a way that other partners had not been able; to trust in love and courage, not fear.

It sounds so constructive, doesn't it? Most of us would agree that if you love someone, you want them to be the most fulfilled and vibrant version of themselves. The reality was trickier, as they soon discovered. There was jealousy on both sides and they hadn't decided how much, and what, information about other dates, sex, relationships they would share. They may have liberated themselves from the confines of a monogamous structure but were without any kind of organising principle under which to shelter, and they were exposed. Bad weather came when Andrea, a year after meeting Anita, started a new and concurrent relationship.

'I'd say we both had to "upskill" and pretty fast. His new girlfriend was prettier, thinner and much younger than me – all the things I had been programmed to believe men wanted. I kept thinking that if he had her then he didn't need me. I had to grapple with so much insecurity – it was agony. I also felt a bit stupid because I had chosen non-monogamy and thought I shouldn't feel jealous,' Anita admits.

It wasn't plain sailing for Andrea either. His new girlfriend shared the same birth week as Anita. When he booked a week away to celebrate with her, the girlfriend felt very hurt and rejected. She expected exactly the same level of birthday attention from Andrea that Anita had received, since she was, after all, his girlfriend too. In the mind of this young woman the set-up was disjointed, and yet to both Anita and Andrea the two relationships were incomparable, one having just begun and the other with a pre-established depth, where the attachment had already grown. Perhaps if Andrea's newer girlfriend also had another relationship, things might have balanced out. But she didn't. She did not really want one either. Truth was, she just wanted Andrea. And for him to just want her. Which was, of course, a problem.

The situation deteriorated over another twelve months, after which things ended with Andrea and his new girlfriend. It was also a very explosive period for Anita and Andrea, who had to a) *un*learn many of their pre-conceived ideas of how to behave in relationships and b) learn how to communicate in a successful open relationship. The time they had together just felt so strained. It almost seemed as though it wasn't worth it, but something kept them hanging on.

Anita told me: 'We screwed up constantly. But we also picked each other up, dusted the relationship off, fixed it, worked with it, changed it and moved on. Until the next screw-up, of course. It was messy, really messy, but the truth is that making any change, or dealing with a new significant other in your significant other's life, is chaotic. The big thing was that we gave each other permission to make mistakes. It definitely made us closer.'

Dealing with a new significant other in your significant other's life. Even the phrase sounds confusing, let alone the reality. Listening to Anita talk about this torturous phase of her relationship with Andrea, I couldn't help wondering: was it worth it? At what point do struggle and heartache outweigh the prize of sexual and mental liberation?

Regardless of whether you like or hate the sound of Anita and Andrea's relationship set-up, they were entitled to make their choices. Besides, there are admirable aspects of their relationship that people with completely different structures could still learn from. Those in consciously non-monogamous relationships have to talk about seemingly taboo things that many people – especially those who are unconsciously monogamous – rarely talk about. Yet we should all be communicating about desire, boundaries, needs and hurt as honestly and sensitively as we can. Anita and Andrea's approach to failure, too, is uplifting: the idea that they might give one another 'permission to make mistakes' is an ingenious subversion of the assumption that mistakes should be avoided, mitigated or at the very least regretted. Not only does it allow for imperfection, but it also builds on it – incredible alchemy that leads to something stronger.

Five years of mistakes later and Anita and Andrea were still committed to both non-monogamy and one another. Both of them still dated other people but did so less frequently, in order to maintain the balance they'd created in their relationship. They also had a better system of what sensitive information to share, and when. Now they could send a message right then and there:

> *Hey darling, hope you're having a lovely evening. I've met someone in the bar and I'm going home with him/her. Call you in the morning. Love you xx*

What they've discovered, after trying things every which way, is that there is never 'a good time' to raise something potentially inflammatory, whereas waiting too long for the 'right time' leaves things to fester unsaid for weeks. Best to 'Just do it', then, in the moment it has happened or arises. After all, this is about making a choice and owning it, knowing the other can do the same. If there is a fallout, then so be it: it won't be lessened by delay.

To the average monogamous mind this sounds outrageous. Even for Anita and Andrea, getting to sleep after receiving a text like that could be difficult, sometimes impossible. What they discovered, however, was that feeling jealous, investigating the source of that jealousy and then being honest about it with each other, could lead to deeper trust and connection. Knowing from experience that they could work through difficulties and emerge intact has made them more resilient. It also allows them to stay conscious, able to continually renegotiate boundaries and reassess where they are *now*.

'There is no set prescription about how often we see each other or how we spend our time when we see each other. It depends on what we each need. One week we'll really miss each other and see each other three times a week, the next not at all because we just need time alone or are stressed with work. Sometimes we walk, sometimes we have sex, sometimes we do both, or neither – whatever. We don't live together, which suits us both. But there is also lots of commitment. It is a less conditional and more conscious commitment, certainly, than I put into my marriage.'

And so, the million-dollar question: is Anita *happier* living this way?

'I think that happiness comes and goes, really, like all feelings, so I don't know about that, but I've definitely experienced a lot more joy in the last five years than ever before. The difference is that now I am aware that I actually have choices. I know when I am choosing something, and I don't feel weighed down by things the way I used to. The relationships I have now, whether romantic or platonic, are based on absolute emotional honesty and are much deeper. Tuning in to my own needs and feelings, and being receptive to other people's needs and feelings, allows for so much more true kindness. It just feels like a whole other level of relating. There is no way that I'd go back,' Anita proudly concludes.

Conscious Choice – In Essence

Conscious choice is any decision or action that has been given some thought before it's taken. It is explicitly related to embracing freedom rather than fear. An *action* and not a *reaction:* never knee-jerk or defensive. It respects the interdependence of human beings, and neither approves of nor endorses excessive dependence or anti-dependence. It's also about losing that internal chatter that says you *should* be doing something, and instead explores what you *could* be doing. Conscious choices can, but do not have to, mean going against the grain. You can consciously make the same choices as many, or consciously choose something unusual.

Conscious Choice – Inquiry

Can you remember the last time you made a very definite conscious choice about something in your life? Try to think of at least two examples, one slightly more trivial (e.g. cutting out carbs or booking a holiday) and one that feels of great importance (e.g. opting to stop your fertility treatment, or finally taking off your wedding ring).

Now try to think of five things you have done in your life on autopilot/unconsciously, following a blueprint or because you *should*. Again, try to find a mix of more minor and major examples. Note these down somewhere private, and/or share them with someone you trust.

Do you see any patterns here? If so, what sense do you make of them?

Now What?

Let it percolate. That's it, really. Now that you've opened, or re-opened, your mind to the idea of conscious choice, just let it filter in. Hopefully you'll have a few light-bulb moments over the next few days/weeks/months, noting the times in your past when you missed choices or looking at your present situation with a fresh perspective. Do make a note of any resistance that crops up, and look for patterns in why and when defeatism or self-limiting beliefs emerge. If this all sounds a bit esoteric, don't worry. In the next chapter we'll bring it all alive as we look more specifically at choice in relationships and hear about those who have chosen non-blueprint paths.

CHAPTER 2

CHOICE AND RELATIONSHIPS

'The Sheep in Wolf's Clothing' – *Alex's Story**

'I realised that having many partners did not have to reduce the quality of each relationship. In fact, it could enhance it.'

Alex was thirty-three when he told his mother he was polyamorous. She took the information in, wondering what it all meant, but didn't ask much at the time. A few years later, she asked a question: 'So, Alex . . . Just *how many* girlfriends do you have right now?'

He answered, 'Well, Mum. That's a hard question to answer because when you say "girlfriend", I know you're making a series of assumptions about what that word means. Are you referring to how many women I'm sleeping with frequently, or would this include someone I might have sex with once every six months, if at all? Is it about who I spend most of my time outside work with, or who I have the strongest romantic feelings about? Because at this point in time I think the answer might be different for each of those questions.'

Alex's mother frowned. She thought a little, and then said, 'Well, who do you spend most of your time with, and have a romantic sexual relationship with?'

Alex thought a while. 'I *suppose* that would be Jean.'

Alex's mother, then in her sixties, nodded. He watched, half smiling, as her shoulders dropped and her breathing slowed. Clearly, she was relieved, having assimilated the information she'd been given and concluded that her son, although he was sleeping with 'a few' women, had just one 'real' girlfriend. This was not ideal, but manageable. She could conceive of it, somehow.

Alex understood her need to make sense of his choices in the only way she knew how, the way that fitted her relationship blueprint. It was a completely different model: she and Alex's father fell in love at high school and had stayed together ever since. They seemed very much in love, their relationship symbiotic, and they still bickered like teenagers. As a result, although the household Alex grew up in was politically liberal, with a strong feminist bent, the 'love paradigm' was still traditional.

It was with this blueprint that Alex moved from Tel Aviv to London, almost two decades ago, when he was twenty-six. Here he hoped to galvanise both his career and his love life. In the former he did well, quickly becoming successful in management consultancy. The latter was trickier, however, as Alex struggled with shyness and found it hard to approach women. It was a lonely time for him, and a culture shock as well. In Israeli culture, where directness is favoured, he had been viewed as a subtle communicator – polite to a fault – whereas in England people clearly found him brash. All of this, combined with his earnestness in matters of romance, meant that for years he struggled to hit it off with the typical twenty-something English female. Eventually, aged twenty-nine, Alex started dating a woman he adored, who was also Israeli. They stayed together for three years, during which time they also got engaged. It was, in many ways, the perfect union except for one, ever-present problem – the thorny issue of sex, and their differing attitudes towards its role in a relationship.

For Alex, working towards mutual sexual contentment was a fundamental part of a successful relationship, whereas his fiancée saw sexual satisfaction merely as a symptom – a positive thing that might occur if they were to sort out their various other issues.

'I remember walking around feeling hungry like a wolf. I didn't know what to do with all my desire. It wasn't that we didn't have sex, but that she did not value it like me. We tried to coast along. Like lots of couples, I think, we relied on our strong romantic love to get us through and so ignored lots of other conflicts.'

In the background, however, both parties felt, in different ways, neglected. Resentment grew. Alex hated who he was becoming. His partner didn't like herself either. They decided marriage was off the cards and separated.

It was in the wake of this relationship that Alex had his first encounter with a dating site, one which suggested people connect with one another according to their answers to certain key questions. Here he noticed that he tended to match with women who were bisexual, non-monogamous and kinky. That he might suit a more 'alternative' person was surprising and now that he was in his early thirties with more self-confidence and self-knowledge, he followed his curiosity. During the Edinburgh Festival, he had a fling with a polyamorous woman with whom he spoke a lot about the lifestyle. She was very educated about conscious non-monogamy and Alex found himself questioning his preconceptions around monogamy and 'one true love'. The idea that more than one strong romantic attachment would be like eating too much ice cream and getting belly ache seemed simplistic now, and limiting. More love literally meant *more love.* Love itself was an abundant and endless force. There was no need to hold it back, nor to contain it in some way.

At the time of writing, Alex has been consciously non-monogamous for over thirteen years and is in four established relationships. In order of length but not importance, there is Marcia, a polyamorous woman living in Berlin with whom Alex has been involved for eleven years. The couple see each other about every six months for an intense period of three to four days, although they occasionally connect via video call and work – 1,000 km apart, but also on opposite sides of the desk.

Alex has another girlfriend, Susan, who lives in France and is also polyamorous. This pair have been together for six years and see each other about once a month, for a few days at a time. It is a close relationship, although they don't communicate much between visits. Alex was a stalwart source of support when Susan lost her father, which bonded the two of them deeply.

Next, there is Emma, who lives in London, and they have been involved for four years. Here, the infatuation is still as strong as it was in the beginning, a fact that astonishes and delights Alex daily. This relationship has gone through different phases, starting off as sexual, then becoming platonic (on Emma's part, at least) before moving on to become a sexual-romantic relationship. Most recently, however, it has morphed into a non-sexual, romantic relationship.

'The amount of sex Emma and I have had in four years is about the same as two months in most other relationships I've been in, yet our relationship now is the strongest it's ever been. She is working through some trauma, and currently wants to be asexual. We cuddle lots, but don't kiss. I'm completely and utterly in love with her.'

The fourth and most recent addition to Alex's relationship smorgasbord is Claire. She is his most frequent sexual partner; somebody he sees every ten days or so and communicates a lot with in between. The relationship is erotic, loving and romantic.

'We have a kinky "vanilla-choc-chip" style,' he explains ('vanilla' meaning largely non-kinky but with some added 'choc-chip'/kink occasionally). 'Claire also has a more hardcore kinky relationship with someone else. I care about her deeply; we love each other, and I would say we are *in love*, but it's a very specific type of relationship because there is a power dynamic going on both inside and outside of the sex we have. It's funny, because before I met Claire I would have thought that this level of total infatuation would inevitably have been a bit clingy and codependent, but because she identifies as a relationship anarchist and is non-monogamous, it does not feel enmeshed in any way, which is amazing.'

Sometimes Emma will come over to his place – a maisonette in Central London – and stay for a few days, the two of them working companionably on different levels, and meeting for lunch, dinner, cuddles and sleep in between. Both Claire and Emma receive stockings from Alex at Christmas, something he would be happy to provide for Susan and Marcia, too, if they chose to come and spend some time in the UK during the holidays.

'The stockings thing makes it sound a bit "kitchen table poly"', referring to a style of polyamory where all the partners have relationships with each other (sexual or non-sexual) and share space with one another. 'That's not what we have because although Susan and Emma are very friendly with each other, the others don't know each other, and I see them all separately. Interestingly, Emma spoke to me once about how her trust in me deepened when she saw me with another girlfriend and realised that I was respectful and kind to both of them.'

That's an interesting dynamic, isn't it? One of the greatest pleasures of polyamory, and also perhaps one of the biggest struggles, is the potential of seeing one's lover with another. Clearly, much of whether this is successful depends on how well handled it is, and how experienced each person is.

It may also depend on whether one is predisposed towards non-monogamy. Can everybody live this way and be fulfilled? I don't think so. There is a level of emotional energy and investment that is required to hold down four committed relationships. Some people don't have it, and others don't want to give it. Love may be in abundance, of course, but time and energy are not, and in giving so much to many romantic connections does one inevitably give less elsewhere? As a parent of a very bouncy little boy, for example, I know for absolute certain that I could not maintain this number of committed sexual-romantic relationships *and* work *and* run a home *and* enjoy close friendships without completely neglecting my child. One choice impacts another choice. It becomes a question of priorities.

In Alex's case, here is a man who has no immediate dependants, a huge appetite for love, and is able to continually offer time and energy to all of his partners without feeling too depleted or strung out. But is there also jealousy, I wonder, either on the part of his girlfriends towards each other or on Alex's part towards their other relationships? Very rarely, is the answer. Provided visits and meet-ups are planned well in advance, there is no need for anyone to be upset or made to feel unimportant.

Does Alex have capacity for anything else, I wonder, noticing my own feelings of panic at the thought? Would he stop at four relationships only? I remember, from my own period of polyamory, finding two quite overwhelming. It depends on the individual and their desires, or the wider context of their lives. But still, there is the question: how much sex and love will be enough? At what point does romance become addictive? Alex does not see his life this way. His relationships are a source of security, not insecurity. He knows he *could* do more, and regularly flirts with the idea of a new, primarily sexual connection with a sporadic lover. Nothing more time-consuming than that, however. Not at the moment, anyway.

As he is a white, heterosexual male in four loving relationships, three of which feel intensely sexual and romantic, it might be easy to judge Alex; on first glance, his relationship setup might be seen to represent the aggressive freedom of the patriarchy, or something sinister about white privilege. Yet this would be to miss the point entirely, I think, like using only the word *circle* to describe the sun. Not only are Alex's girlfriends just as free to pursue other relationships and connections as he is, but there is also nothing that seems avaricious or dominating in the way Alex moves through the world. In fact, he is an incredibly thoughtful person, whose behaviour towards the women close to him is almost unfailingly respectful and tender. He has also remained friends with almost all of his exes – not a common thing– which strikes me as another nod towards his non-traditional view of relationships and his ability to manage change and communicate well.

Perhaps it is in witnessing or hearing about this kind of diligent commitment to every intimate relationship that has meant Alex's mother has come around lately – some ten years after learning about Alex's polyamory and six years since asking *that question* – to understanding more fully her son's chosen way of life. She might not have chosen it *for* him, and certainly did not choose it for herself, but she no longer fears polyamory in the way she once did. Instead, she accepts that Alex currently has four girlfriends, each of whom he loves and desires in a very different and unique way.

But not everyone takes this journey towards tolerance and understanding. Many people, in fact, refuse to. They are either mentally rigid, unable to conceive of an alternative relationship paradigm, or they are arrogant in their viewpoint, refusing to believe that something wildly different from their setup might work for another person. As a result, Alex chooses not to be 'out' very much – certainly not at work or with more conservative friends. There are no benefits to it, he insists. Rather the opposite, as he is often judged, shamed and belittled.

'I once came out to two childhood friends, a heterosexual couple who had been together since they were teens and were now married to each other. The woman in particular was very damning and said some things that I found hurtful. I think she was afraid that I was telling her husband that he was a sucker for being monogamous and could be having sex with so many more women! I remember thinking at the time that, if I had come out to them as gay, it would have been better received.'

I have heard so many similar stories to this one. Unconsciously monogamous people tend to judge polyamory far more harshly than they would many other lifestyle decisions, such as going to live off-grid or opting to be vegan. Something about the choice to be openly non-monogamous forces monogamous couples to examine their choices in a way that is often perceived as threatening. The polyamorist becomes 'the taker', emblematic of something greedy and amoral. Of course, sometimes this is the case. There is no identity or lifestyle choice that will totally prohibit a person from being a complete arsehole; you can give half your earnings to charity and still act unpleasantly to other people. Yet it is mostly true that those drawn to polyamory go through just as much, if not more, difficult stuff in relationships than monogamous folks, including rejection, disappointment and heartbreak.

'One thing that's happened quite a lot is that I'll meet someone who has never tried conscious non-monogamy but really likes the idea of it. They try it, with me and others, and start to evangelise on non-monogamy. Then, about six months down the line, they meet a heteronormative monogamous dude, and in spending time with him they remember how much they miss all the social privilege that comes with being "normal". So they go back to monogamy and I get my heart broken.'

Alex does not say this with self-pity. He is well aware that in pursuing multiple relationships he leaves himself open to both more love and more loss. The point here is that there are always aspects of a person's life and choices that we are probably not privy to. (Even as a therapist, I can sit opposite a client who appears to be telling me all about their inner world and feel I know them intimately, and yet I never see them as a parent, or at work, or watch the way they interact in the pub.) There is always more to learn about someone. We must not assume we know it all.

With Alex, there are many layers. There is another important part of his story that I have held back thus far, unsure of its precise relevance to his romantic life. Yet to omit it feels like a betrayal, because Alex is also a survivor of sexual abuse – a very grim and visceral kind of exploitation that took place from when he was ten. The perpetrator, someone in his extended family, was an older man that Alex looked up to, as well as a well-respected member of the community. The abuse stopped when he reached twelve ('as I wised up', he says), after which he fell into a persistent state of chronic depression.

When Alex was seventeen, he confided in his mother about what had happened. It was not until he was twenty-one, however, that he sought therapeutic help and then, a couple of years later, reported the abuse.

There followed the ravages of a police inquiry and trial. In the end, Alex's abuser was found guilty and sentenced to six months' community service. It was both baffling and distressing that this man should receive such an unremarkable punishment, especially since the inquiry had uncovered another of this man's victims. Although this other case did not go to trial, it was the fact of having his own experience validated by another that began to help Alex heal. Gradually he was released from the slaughter of self-doubt and the ravages of shame, although, of course, the scars remain.

'I'm what you might call a gender traitor – somebody who is trying to fight the good fight against toxic masculinity. I was hurt by it. The guy who abused me, besides obviously being a paedophile, was also a closeted homosexual married to a lesbian in a marriage of convenience. He was probably an abuse survivor as well. The world is fucked. It's how those things work – pain just persists.'

Pain just persists. In my experience as a therapist, this is so often the case: victims become persecutors and perpetuate the tragic cycle of abuse that they swore to themselves they would never repeat, until one day someone is able, thanks to both fortune and bravery, to tread a different path. Alex freely admits that the trauma of his abuse, combined with his dreamy, big-hearted nature, could be two important factors among many in his polyamory – his feeling more satiated when encircled by many deep connections rather than merely one.

I question, really, how much this matters. We are all the sum of our experiences, aren't we? Alex freely admits that he felt 'kind of broken' by the abuse and that, perhaps yes, he does crave romance as a kind of salve. And my response is, *Okay, so?* Some things come from darkness, and some things come from light. What matters most is our awareness, and also what we do with it. If the setup works for Alex and his partners, then can there really be a problem? There is something about the way that Alex is living, loving and healing that feels both courageous *and* self-protective; both very adult *and* adolescent. This paradox makes complete sense to me, since both professionally and personally I am regularly struck by the way our younger selves stay with us as we age. Our past is always in our present. Yet it is also in the past. Is this a nonsensical contradiction? Maybe. But human beings are full of them, and our relationships are too.

Beyond the Blueprint – A Range of Other Styles

Now that we've established that there is a world beyond that supposed gold-standard monogamous long-term relationship, let's take a look at some other options. This is not an exhaustive list, but it does include the most common types of relationship radicalism that go beyond the blueprint. Some of these things may seem obvious, and others more alien. A few of the models listed here, as you'll notice, are more about creating a different blueprint than they are about rejecting the idea completely.

Here's a slight disclaimer: there will inevitably be people who read these descriptions and disagree with aspects of them, because a) the language around non-monogamy and relationships is constantly evolving and b) this is a simplistic view and the many self-confessed 'relationship geeks' will want a much more nuanced view. Think of the descriptions below as a way of kitting you out just well enough (in a pair of sturdy wellies) so that you can go wandering into the land of conscious relationship building, and then upgrade your gear later on (to high-tech walking boots) with other reading.

Conscious monogamy

The difference between conscious monogamy and unconscious monogamy is like the difference between sitting down to enjoy some chocolate cake, mindfully and without guilt, and standing in front of the fridge shoving cake into your mouth because you're bored. Unconscious monogamy – by which I mean falling into monogamy as a default – remains a central feature of our society's relationship blueprint. What is less frequently discussed is conscious monogamy: making the decision to have just one sexual partner at a time in full awareness that there are other viable and respectable options. Here, two people actively agree, from a place of choice and freedom rather than guilt or duty, to be exclusive.

Non-monogamy – conscious and unconscious

Non-monogamy is an umbrella term. It can be used to refer to a number of different relationship structures that are all 'non-dyadic' in some way, i.e. not having to involve just two.

Unconscious (or unethical) non-monogamy: We could just call this *fucking around.* If you are living a non-monogamous life without telling your partner(s) about it, or if you're open about your non-monogamy but taking no care whatsoever over anybody's feelings or boundaries, then you are unethically non-monogamous. In many ways, this form of non-monogamy, which very often equates to cheating, is in the shadow of the blueprint. It happens frequently, and seems less alien to many than the choice to adopt an ethically non-monogamous stance. Yet it comes with a clear sting. Full-scale cheating, although often charged and dynamic, is a destructive act that will likely (and I say this with love and from experience) cause stress and heartbreak.

Conscious (or ethical) non-monogamy: Let's call this *fucking around responsibly.* If you are more cognisant of your non-monogamous actions, and particularly if you are willing to take responsibility for them, then you are being more ethically and consciously non-monogamous, and will probably end up happier. You may still get your heart broken, though (I also say this from experience). That is just part of living love.

Open relationship: An open relationship is *any relationship that allows for a degree of fucking around.* The 'open' part only refers to the *what* and not the *how,* so can be done more or less ethically, depending on who does it. The degree to which a relationship is actually 'open' can differ and change wildly between people, as can the specific policies agreed by those within open relationships. I used to joke years ago that my relationship with B was 'ajar' rather than fully open or closed because we had made reference to the potentiality for extramarital sexual adventures but never fully discussed or sanctioned it. (Warning: this is a recipe for disaster. There are too many blanks left open for each partner to fill regarding what the other partner will or won't be okay with.)

Non-monogamy and open relationships – specific subsets, terms, structures

Here are some of the most prevalent styles of non-monogamy, which often come with their own sets of norms and expectations.

Monogamish: This is a term created by the American relationships columnist and podcaster Dan Savage. It means mostly-monogamous-but-sometimes-not. The 'ish' is about making allowances, and being realistic about possibilities, rather than a lack of commitment to the central relationship.

Swingers: This used to refer to couples who enjoy 'swinging' – that is, swapping sexual partners with other couples. The British media seems to be obsessed by swinging for some reason, which is often the subject of scandalous headlines as if it were the only kind of adult sexual activity that does not fit the blueprint!

Hall pass: Some relationships are closed except for allowing for the occasional 'hall pass', which refers to a one-off or very occasional sexual experience with someone outside of the primary relationship.

'Don't ask, don't tell' (DADT): Meaning, *You can fuck who you want but I don't want to know about it.* Some people (including me) consider this option to be in direct conflict with the conscious part of conscious non-monogamy because it demands a level of secrecy. Yet it remains a widely common arrangement among long-term relationships and marriages throughout history.

Polyamory: The word 'polyamory' is a mishmash of the Greek and the Latin meaning *many* and *love*. It's having the capacity for multiple romantic attachments at once with the consent of all the people involved. Networks of people connected via polyamorous relationships are called 'polycules', and groups of people who agree to remain in sexual-romantic relationships only with each other (closed groups) are called 'polyfidelitous'.

Polyamory is one subset of conscious non-monogamy and has various different subsets of its own, including, for example, 'hierarchical polyamory', which means that relationships are placed in a specific hierarchical structure to reflect their importance. In this instance people might have a primary partner and a secondary and tertiary partner. The primary one is usually the one they might share living space, finances, children with, etc. Non-hierarchical polyamory is, as its name suggests, the practice of multiple relationships without any kind of order of importance attached to them.

Polyamory, as an identity, tends to be chosen by those who engage in a deeper and more long-term intimacy with their multiple partners, rather than those who choose to call themselves consciously non-monogamous. Solo poly is engaging in relationships while never being in a couple at all. This is similar to, but not the same as, Relationship Anarchy (see page 49). Confused? That's okay – it all overlaps a bit and can take a while to get your head around. Just don't make the cardinal mistake of assuming polyamory is the same as polygamy – this pissed me off disproportionately when I was polyamorous! Polyamory is a way of being as well as a relationship status, and requires all parties to consent. Polygamy is often duplicitous. It means to be married to more than one person and is illegal in many countries (an offence referred to as bigamy).

Relationship Anarchy

I suppose this could go under the umbrella of non-monogamy, but I feel it deserves a standalone segment since, by its nature, it defies categorisation and is a holistic attitude to relationships.

The term 'relationship anarchy' (RA) is found in Andie Nordgren's 2006 essay 'The short instructional manifesto for relationship anarchy', originally in Swedish, and means applying the principles of anarchy to intimate relationships. In some ways, the word 'anarchy' is a bit unhelpful, as we might infer chaos. In fact, relationship anarchists are often very ordered in their thinking and mindful in their choices. They will almost certainly have spent a lot of time and effort thinking about the structure and content of a relationship – much more time, usually, than those in monogamous relationships.

RA is more about refuting the idea that monogamy is 'normal' than it is about rejecting monogamy itself. At its core, it is a rejection of any pecking order. RA does away with the notion that romantic relationships differ from friendships. It is based on the premise that we all possess the capacity to love more than one person and that love takes many forms.

The main thrust of RA is that all relationships are unique and to automatically or unconsciously value one specific type over another, or to typecast them at all, is to undermine the individuality of each particular bond; that assigning value is a result of social conditioning rather than conscious choice. In essence: the rules are, there are no rules. Except to be conscious and self-aware.

Conscious Non-monogamy (CNM) – Things to Watch Out For

CNM is not about *having it all,* whenever you want, however you want it. It is not really about *having* at all, because it acknowledges that no person has guaranteed ownership over another. CNM is not about trying to have the best bits of relationships without any compromise or challenge. It actually involves arguably more of the tricky stuff than any kind of monogamy. There are no rules about who or what you must be, sexually, in order to be consciously non-monogamous. Your sexuality in general is merely a detail of who you are and not an essential requirement for entry.

CNM is fundamentally about possibilities. It responds to a desire to have more options in one's relationships. CNM is more about *could* than *should*. It requires flexibility and does not rule out commitment either. It is not necessarily a behaviour but can refer to a belief system: one can behave monogamously while maintaining a belief in the principle of conscious non-monogamy.

CNM is closer to a well-considered, long-term lifestyle choice than a quick fix. It reflects something *that can keep changing* about identity and principles. Obviously sex features, but far less than many think. Those who really embrace the possibility of CNM usually regard it, first and foremost, as a mindset or belief system that may happen to involve sexual non-exclusivity, in the same way that real-deal yogis regard yoga as a mindset or belief system, rather than just the physical practice of postures.

To allow more choice to be present within relationships, we need to build those relationships consciously. That is essentially what the term 'conscious relationship building' (CRB) refers to: building relationships with others and oneself from a mindful, self-aware and embodied place. It suggests a sense of being awake within those key relationships in your life, and making decisions from that attentive, purposeful place. It can be adopted and enacted by those who identify as monogamous, non-monogamous, polyamorous, kinky, vanilla, sex positive, asexual – whatever. It's for everyone.

Conscious relationships are an ongoing process. I like to think of them as something you actively *do* rather than are just *in*. They are not something you build once and which then take care of themselves.

We are constantly adapting, changing and evolving, and so too are our relationships. CRB is for people who are prepared to have uncomfortable conversations, lean into challenging experiences and feel the blood pumping through their veins. It is for people for whom truth and freedom are primary values, and for those who treasure their relationships. I genuinely believe that if more people were shown how to courageously lean into such discomfort, there would be fewer acrimonious divorces, traumatic custody battles, sibling feuds and other long-standing resentments that cause chronic stress and misery.

So why aren't we all more conscious in our approach to relationships? Because it's hard, basically. Also, we grow up with the idea rammed down our throats that love is all you really need to make something work. Not true at all. In fact, we need to be able to develop an array of qualities and skills that can take time and effort to learn.

The ideas in this book may change the way you think about relationships. They might attract or annoy you, *and that's good.* Either you are learning what you feel about an idea or you are learning where you are blocked. In these instances, you are being challenged to go beyond yourself and at least look from another perspective. This takes humility and guts, as there is no more important work you can do (for your relationships) than getting to know yourself. Then, the magic happens.

The Relationship Escalator

The precise origin of this term is a bit of a mystery, though according to Amy Gahran, whose book, *Stepping Off the Relationship Escalator: Uncommon Love and Life,* was published in 2017, it has been increasingly used in the consensually non-monogamous community since 2010.

The relationship escalator is a metaphor used to describe one major aspect of our society's relationship blueprint, which is that it is all about explicit progression. The escalator signifies passivity: the only effort required is to step on at the bottom and one is carried to the top.

The widespread belief is that, in order to be successful and mature, a relationship should move in one direction only ('The only way is up, baby!' as I used to belt out from my bedroom, repeating the only lyrics anyone can remember from the 1988 smash-hit single by Yazz and the Plastic Population). The designated stages will vary a little, but on the whole the escalator takes us through a seemingly linear progression that Gahran refers to as making contact (flirting, dates), initiation (romantic courtship), claiming and defining (declarations of love and exclusivity), establishment (settling patterns of communication and time together), commitment (making long-term plans as a monogamous couple), merging (of finances, property, families), conclusion (getting married) and legacy (e.g. buying a home and having children).

This is recognisable, right? For those for whom this is familiar, it may also have been automatic. How long have you cruised through life thinking the escalator model is/was the best or only way of approaching so-called 'proper' romantic relationships? Most of us aren't exposed to much else. But take a moment to ask yourself *why* . . . *Why* is it, actually, that the *only* way is up? And what does it even mean to go upwards? This implies there is a top point that one should reach. Why can't 'up' just mean getting closer to someone emotionally, having better sex or just feeling like things are good enough? Why should we move in any specific direction at all, come to think of it? And why, oh why, must friends and family constantly ask you about when you're going to get *the ring*? Or when they will hear the *pitter-patter of tiny feet*? When you really step back and question it, you might see how many of the things most of us spout about what a relationship *should* look like is little more than a large serving of social conditioning with a dollop of existential angst.

The other issue with the escalator is that when you get to the top, you've got nowhere to go. If success is marriage, children, owning your own property/car/second home and reaching your twenty-fifth wedding anniversary without having killed each other, then what emphasis are you placing on personal growth? This model also assumes you definitely *want* or need to reach the top. Maybe you find yourself happy in the dating stage and want to stay there. Why do we pay such attention to any *next* step? Besides, when you consider that we live in a world with a very high divorce rate and no need for further population, it seems a mystery that so many of us clamour towards marriage and having children.

I am not anti-progression, I promise, nor am I against including structure in the way one thinks of relationships. But I also believe that relationships are 360 degrees in scope, which means they are inevitably limited in their movement if we are busy going up or down an escalator. Think about when we hear that a couple who used to live together has decided to live separately. For the vast majority of people, their first reaction is invariably: *Are they splitting up?* Then, if the answer is no, there is confusion – a similar kind of confusion as one might experience upon hearing that, after thirty years of living and loving together, a couple are finally getting married. *Why not earlier?* most people ask. Separation is another one. We tend to assume it is always bad and we immediately use the word 'break-up'. But what if it was not just about 'breaking' one thing, but about building something else? What if the separation could be seen as yet another shift? A normal, often painful part of many relationships is when people's feelings for each other change. Yes, change is hard, though it can be positive. So do we have to call it failure? Surely this just adds yet more pressure. Why must we be so binary?

All assumptions should be questioned every now and again, a bit like having a clothes clear-out, just to assess what still fits. Here's a provocative example: why is marriage forever? These days, it seems outdated to stick to a term in a contract when so many other conditions have changed. We live far longer and in a completely different world to those a few centuries back, where women, in particular, have access to a great deal more financial freedom. In an article that she wrote for the *Guardian*, author and journalist Jeanette Winterson proposed a fixed term for marriage;

that instead the parties agreed to a specific amount of time. As I read it, I found myself laughing, railing against it and thinking, *Marriage, a fixed term? But that defies the whole point!* 'Why?' I asked myself. *Because it's marriage – it's forever.* 'Why,' I asked again, 'when so many marriages end in divorce, often unplanned and mishandled?' *Because marriage is about an ideal. It's about at least trying to do forever.* 'Why?' I asked again. 'Why should something as important as marriage be based on a lofty ideal that, clearly, few of us can maintain and even fewer manage with fulfilment?' *Because marriage . . .*

I couldn't answer. Instead, I took a little while to imagine how it might have been if my own civil partnership had been entered into as a renewable ten-year-long, fixed-term agreement. I wondered how I might have behaved differently and made less desperate choices. Perhaps I might have felt less terrified when things weren't going well, and felt more able, paradoxically, to communicate better. Certainly, the end of our sexual-romantic relationship would have been less traumatic if we were able to celebrate the success of having reached our ten-year renewal date (and merely decided to leave it there, thanking one another for a rich and meaningful decade), rather than feeling we had completely failed at *forever*. And who knows? We might also have been more prepared for the logistical, financial and emotional dismantling that was to come once we decided to separate.

The biggest problem with starting to open minds and hearts to relationships 'off the escalator' is the negative connotations that pervade. At least 80 per cent of the time when I speak to people it quickly becomes clear that they assume the decision to change the structure of any relationship comes from a place of dissatisfaction, rather than curiosity and security. The assumption itself is largely unconscious, and it is only when questioned directly that the bias, and the potential for any other perspective, is revealed.

Such an assumption isn't always wrong, I should add. There *are* couples who come to CNM as a way of fixing the broken bits in their existing relationship. This rarely works, though. CNM won't paper over cracks in any relationship (as Anita and ex-husband Marc hoped it might); it could instead illuminate them. Yet there are also people who adopt a more open style of relationship precisely because they feel secure enough to explore. This latter story is often overlooked because it goes against so much of what we are taught about commitment. When it is done in a mindful, conscious way, many people/couples find that having a more flexible approach to relationship structures actually encourages more connection. If you are looking to renovate anything (be it a house or a relationship), the question of whether the foundations will withstand the change is pretty crucial.

Beware the Sacrificial 'Either/Or' Mentality

The prevailing notion seems to be that making a choice to go after one thing means necessarily losing another.

In an adult world, however, we face the reality that we simply cannot enjoy everything we want, all of the time. At some point, we all learn that we cannot have the safety and friendship inherent in many committed relationships without compromising at least a little on our own longings. Very often we mistake compromise with self-sacrifice. Sometimes we even learn, or tell ourselves, that our basic needs are too much, and that to want them met in a relationship is just 'silly'.

In fact, it is precisely this denial of our needs that leads to conflict. Think of it like a stringent diet, where the denial of hunger results in something destructive and self-defeating, like a massive binge before a penitent restart. In relationships, this negating of needs and wants can manifest in destructive ways, such as sexual transgressions or withholding, co-dependency or emotional shutdown.

I am absolutely *not* saying that you can do whatever you like in a relationship. It is, of course, the case that in any real, sustainable relationship we do have to compromise sometimes on what we want now, in favour of what we want overall; often we are required to zoom out and take stock. But that's still a choice. It doesn't necessitate self-sacrifice. After all, why must we choose quite so absolutely between security and adventure? Who told you having both wasn't an option? In fact, the path with both *is there*; it is a bit harder, but it is also beautiful and worthwhile.

To put it another way: if unconscious monogamy is about *either/or*, then conscious relationship building is about *and*. It is less a success or failure, and more a continual process of nurture and evaluation, of rebuilding and growth.

'Circles of Choice' – *Hannah's Story*

'I've no interest in the idea of growing old with a husband or wife. As a queer person with an unconventional approach to relationships, finding people I fancy who have similar values is like fishing in a teaspoon.'

Hannah, forty-four, describes herself as queer and solo. 'Queer', she says, denotes a total rejection of hetero- and amato-normativity,* not just around gender and sexuality, but also how she does relationships. 'Solo' means she's at the centre of a constellation of different types of relationships, having decided against coupledom as an organising principle. She also jokingly calls herself 'post-monogamous' because, although Hannah has now been non-monogamous for the last decade, prior to that she was monogamous.

The way Hannah lives in relationships is about as far removed from the average person as it gets. It is not that she doesn't value relationships – far

* Arizona State University professor of philosophy Elizabeth Brake used this term to capture societal assumptions about romance: https://elizabethbrake.com/amatonormativity/

from it – just that she doesn't automatically adhere to any of the normal structures that fit the blueprint most of us know best. 'The relationships which feel "intimate" to me are the ones where there is mutual, informed consent, mutual vulnerability and a mutual commitment to own and work on our shit. These relationships may be long- or short-standing, they may or may not have involved sex or "romance". For example, one of my most intimate relationships is with my brother. The popular imagination that sex is what makes a relationship "intimate" erases many other kinds of relationships that help meet our need to feel known, while unduly centring on a particular subset of relationships, among which, sadly, the qualities I've described are very often absent.'

In many ways Hannah is an emblem of conscious choice, having constructed her own interpersonal blueprint, not to mention a specific lifestyle. It wasn't always this way, though. Hannah was born in London to white, middle-class parents who were professional but not wealthy. Her childhood involved a few moves around the country, and after university she returned to London, where she worked for fifteen years in a corporate job. For fourteen years Hannah was also in a monogamous relationship with a woman who did not share her belief that monogamy is quite an old ideal. For most of their time together Hannah was keener on her girlfriend than she was on pursuing CNM.

It was a wonderfully spacious, loving and, for the most part, intentional relationship. Still, the big issue of monogamy hung around. Every three years or so, Hannah would raise the subject of 'seeing other people' again, just to see if there was any chance of renegotiation. But no: her girlfriend was quite clear, sobbing at the very thought of 'opening up'.

'We really wanted it to work, but . . . if you imagine two hands cupped together around an orange. That container was our relationship. It had expanded and expanded, and it just couldn't expand any more and still contain us both.'

Hannah's sexuality and sense of self had started spilling over. 'We tried very carefully and kindly to work out if there was some way to keep aspects of our relationship and also allow it to change, but in the end I think what we each needed was more different than similar. I couldn't just go off and have don't-ask-don't-tell sexual liaisons and then go back to being contained in a conventional relationship model. She was very clear that she wanted that typical model, and went directly into that in her next relationship, whereas I haven't done anything straightforward since! My ex says she wouldn't like to have such a complicated life, but I'm okay with complicated.'

A few years after this relationship ended by mutual consent, Hannah decided to go totally off-piste. She quit her corporate job, rented out her house and took off for five years into a nomadic lifestyle on her bicycle. If that sounds impulsive, it really wasn't. She had been complaining about her job, the office, the routine, for years. She knew something needed to change, but it was only when her therapist asked her if there was any really good reason why she couldn't just quit that she actually made a choice. She sat down with one of her closest friends and crunched some numbers. If she could manage to live off wild camping and lentil stew, then she could do it. Hannah left the life she knew and headed off towards Portugal. From there she cycled via Corsica, Sardinia, Sicily and the foot of Italy to Greece. She stopped in Lesvos a while to help with the refugee crisis. After a year and a half in Europe, Hannah flew to Canada with her bike and journeyed south, to Mexico, where she started to pick up Spanish before continuing down through South America to Patagonia. Each year several friends and lovers came to visit her en route.

Hannah, who was by now conversant in Spanish, decided to settle in northern Spain, in the capital of Galicia, Santiago de Compostela. After all the travelling, she was ready to base herself somewhere, at least for a while. Settling physically, perhaps, but certainly not back into traditional relationship models. What had become crystal clear throughout her travels was how many of her needs could be met within friendships – most of which do not include a hint of sex. Releasing herself from the blueprint of how any relationship should look allowed Hannah to enjoy a plethora of different types of connections; to thrive off variety. It is her long-term friendships that have become the most central in her life, those special people who have seen her through various twists and turns. Those who are important in Hannah's life orbit around her in concentric circles, according to their emotional proximity and reliability, rather than their role. At the centre of Hannah's current relationship orbit, she puts herself and her future cat! Next, there are the 'nucleus people' – those some people call their 'chosen family' – and then a bunch of other close friends and, lastly, acquaintances. Whether she is having sex or is romantically involved with someone is hardly a deciding factor in how central they are in her circle.

'Perhaps the closest thing I've got to a life partner is a gay man I've known for over twenty-five years. We met at university, then he moved into my street in London with his now-ex-husband, and we've also worked and travelled together. In fact, it's become a running joke that he copies everything I do. He's even learning Spanish and planning to move when he retires. We have contact most days. Since I pulled all the rugs out from under myself, a lot of my friends have been going through midlife crises of their own and I'm happy when, being a few steps down the line, I'm able to support them.'

Whether one shares it or not, there is a great deal of sense in Hannah's philosophy. If we are able to step away from the blueprint, we might ask ourselves why, in this day and age, we ought to value our current sexual or romantic partnerships more highly than our intimate or age-old friendships. Of course, we *can* put the person or people we want to get naked with at the centre of our world, but we don't *have* to.

'Most of my needs are already met in my platonic friendships, old and new. I do get laid, but it's not what I organise my life around.' Right now, Hannah is planning to buy a house with a separate "guest house" for her friends to come and go. 'Lots of them know each other; it's been suggested I set up a Google Calendar so they can deliberately coincide with or indeed avoid each other!' she says.

'Any romantic partners I meet in future will always have just walked through the door. I know it's really tempting to throw oneself into the incredible energy of a new relationship, but what I see people doing all the time is valuing their sexual-romantic relationships so much that they leapfrog to the top of their personal hierarchy,' she points out. 'The friendships get demoted or abandoned. To me, that's a short-sighted, risky strategy. I value enduring bonds the most.'

Choice and Relationships – In Essence

From a choice-ist perspective, there is no designated way of viewing your relationships. Relationships do not have to be placed in a hierarchy. A friendship can be romantic without being sexual, just as a relationship can be sexual but not romantic. You can decide which relationships you put your energy and time into, rather than automatically placing a romantic bond above a friendship in the pecking order or a familial connection above a friendship.

Many people unwittingly step onto the Relationship Escalator (see page 51). This refers to the widespread idea that a decent, committed and fulfilling relationship will follow a series of steps that are seen as progressive. These include dating, cohabiting, marriage and family-making, though they can vary across cultures and generations.

Choice and Relationships – Inquiry

Without thinking too much about it, go ahead and finish the following sentence: *If I wish to enjoy a fulfilling and committed relationship, then I must give up on my . . .*

What did you come up with?

Time? Passion? Freedom? Independence? Career? Autonomy?

It is important to question one's existing beliefs at the start of any self-inquiry, not only because the answers provide you with valuable information, but also because the act of questioning is in itself fundamental to growth. Here are a few questions to get you started:

- What does a successful relationship look like to you?
- What does an unsuccessful relationship look like to you?
- What is working for you right now within your relationship set-up? (This can be answered whatever your situation, whether single or not.) Why?
- What is not working right now? Why?
- Are you feeling resistance to this line of questioning? Like, *This is stupid,* or, *Who really asks themselves such questions?* Maybe these questions make you scared, or excited, or both. That's okay – fear and excitement are blood relatives. They pump through our veins, reminding us we are mortal.

If that line of questioning felt okay, perhaps go a bit further. What are your thoughts on the following?

- What does fidelity mean to you?
- Are commitment and monogamy mutually exclusive? If so, why? If not, why not?

Now What?

Hopefully you've challenged yourself with a few big questions on some of the themes in this chapter, like fidelity and monogamy, and recognised the Relationship Escalator model as *one* way of moving through a relationship, rather than the *only* way. Next, let's zoom in a little, moving away from talking broadly about relationship structures and towards something more specific: the topic of intimacy.

CHAPTER 3

CHOICE AND INTIMACY

Intimate Data – *Dmitri's Story**

'I always assumed that sex was something I would automatically be able to do, just because I had a penis. But that was wrong, as I discovered.'

Dmitri, twenty-nine, is tall and thoughtful, a bright economist who owns his home on the South Coast. He has never had an intimate relationship, nor ever really dated. Thus far, all his sexual experiences have been with sex workers.

'The way I experience the world is fundamentally different from how other people experience the world. Firstly, my brain runs at 100 mph. It's like having a Formula One engine constantly revving in my head. It's difficult and lonely and brings a lot of negatives that other people don't experience or appreciate. I don't have the vernacular, linguistically or emotionally, to engage with people around relationships or modes of courtship. I have to run the script in my head about how to keep conversation going and be engaging and appropriate. Then I get self-conscious, and wonder, *Am I doing the right thing with my eyes? What is their face telling me? Why are they making that expression? Are they happy, or do they just have wind?* There is so much information in real-time that I'm trying to process that it just gets overwhelming. It's all just . . . data, for me to read,' he explains.

All just data. This might sound clinical, perhaps, but it is also how Dmitri's mind works, and part of his high-functioning neurodivergence with Asperger's, which puts him on the autism spectrum. Asperger's affects around 1 per cent of the UK population and is characterised by difficulties in social interaction and understanding non-verbal behaviour – the kind of difficulties that can greatly impact communication, connection and intimacy.

It is not just this that contributes to Dmitri's sense of alienation. 'I'm viewed differently as a brown man,' referring to his South Asian heritage – something he learnt was a problem from a very young age, having grown up in a racist area of Middle England. Even inside the home, there was little modelling of love since his parents' marriage was dysfunctional and unhappy.

'Living in that house was trench warfare. The arguments, the silent treatment that went on for days . . . I knew from the age of four that there was something fundamentally wrong with our household.'

Clearly Dmitri grew up with a distinct lack of environmental safety, both inside and outside the home. It is perhaps no wonder that he struggles to be intimate with others. How can we be intimate without first feeling safe, particularly in our own homes? It is a cruel and commonplace conundrum: those of us who have not experienced healthy intimacy growing up struggle to achieve it as adults, even though it is exactly what we might need to heal. This is partly because when we grow up around chaos and dysfunction, we are even less able to discriminate between what is healthy or unhealthy for us. It is also because allowing oneself to be intimate with another person means to risk triggering whatever trauma took place in early life – our 'early wounding' as it is sometimes called.

Dmitri suffered rejection the first and only time he went on a date. After dinner and a walk, the pair went back to Dmitri's date's place with the intention of having sex. Things did not go quite as planned, however.

'There was very little rapport, and I felt uncomfortable and anxious. My thoughts went fast; there was that whirring in my brain – which meant that I couldn't get aroused, which made me even less relaxed and . . . well. My main sex education was through pornography. I always thought sex was something I'd automatically be able to do, but that was wrong. My date was clearly not impressed, and I left, feeling embarrassed.'

A few days later Dmitri discovered that his date had told all her friends about what had happened. Now his embarrassment rotted into shame and self-disgust. Two years passed, with Dmitri unable to date for fear that something similar would happen. Hope arrived in the form of a newspaper article about surrogate partnership, a specialised area of sex work that includes a therapeutic package where a trained individual engages with a client in a sensitive, focused way in order to help them build sexual confidence. Dmitri nervously called the agency and was referred to a suitable surrogate.

From the first session, it became clear that Dmitri had made a positive choice. Working on physical intimacy in a professional context allowed him to side-step his ever-present anxieties about how to behave. To be intimate we must feel safe, and to feel safe we can't feel judged – not something that a person with Dmitri's background and neurodivergence could achieve with hook-up culture. Thanks to surrogacy, he was able to explore the mechanics of sex and also begin learning how to "do" intimacy. Such intimacy, as it turned out, was the bit he needed most. The part that really nourished him.

Like any education, this process took time and patience. Having established trust in the first session, Dmitri continued to work with this surrogate partner for five more three-hour sessions: the maximum allowed in one block so as to prevent an unhealthy dependency developing between client and surrogate. Each time, he felt he understood a little better what it meant to be physically and emotionally close to another person. Orgasm, however, remained elusive.

Four years and lots of personal development work later, Dmitri contacted the same surrogate and asked if they could meet again. Given the time that had elapsed since their previous session, she agreed. What happened next was transformational.

'There was a lot I had learnt in that first period of exploration – about myself, my body and mindfulness – that I was able to consolidate in this second block of sessions, which are still to this day some of the most intimate experiences I have had with another person. Even though it was boundaried, there was still a deep connection.'

The sessions ended quite perfectly.

'I unexpectedly had an orgasm, which brought a sense of completion to the journey. It was very intense, in a good way, and it's still etched into my mind. It would never have happened without the intimacy, though – the emotional connection we had built.'

Emotional connection. Mindful intimacy. Unexpected, transformational peaks that subtly alter one's narrative of one's own life . . . Listening to Dmitri speak was both humbling and heartening. I was touched to hear of the intimate moments he shared with his sexual surrogate and saddened that this healing side of sex work often gets overshadowed by the darker aspects of the industry, where people are grossly exploited for profit. Despite the obvious benefits to his physical and mental health, Dmitri feels compelled to keep his past surrogacy appointments secret in a way that he doesn't about his psychotherapy. Many of us are more private about our sex lives than any other area, but what if there was no stigma attached to exploring intimacy, in such a boundaried, straightforward context?

So much of what Dmitri talks about gaining from these experiences, after all, resembles what a client might gain from psychotherapy. Minus any sexual contact, I might add. What both sex surrogacy and psychotherapy share is the absolute focus on the client, with a goal of helping them foster a better understanding of themselves and their needs. In terms of subject matter, there is very little that a good therapist would consider out of bounds. Instead, every interaction can simply provide more 'grist to the mill', offering the client another page of their psychic and relational map to unfold, helping them get to know themselves.

What psychotherapy also shares with sexual surrogacy is the potential for great intimacy on the one hand and its transactional nature on the other. Many find this combination problematic, yet there is also something about the exchange of money, for time and expertise, that has the effect of making things safer. In essence, both parties know the deal. Time boundaries too (most psychotherapy sessions are a strict fifty minutes only) create a 'safe container', such that both parties feel held by the clock. It might seem counterintuitive, but consistent boundaries tend to enhance the potential for intimacy, rather than hinder it.

So where does all this leave Dmitri? Since that final session with the surrogate, he has made visits to other sex workers – experiences that he has enjoyed and which have raised his confidence that he can develop intimacy with other, new people. But this is not what he wants forever. Dmitri is adamant that he wants to build on these experiences and integrate intimacy more fully into his life, finding a partner and long-lasting love.

Your Intimacy Blueprint – What Is Intimacy, for You (and Them)?

Intimacy. The official definition is 'the state of having a close, personal relationship or romantic relationship with someone'.* An intimate relationship is usually regarded as containing *either* a physical or emotional closeness, though people tend to use the word to imply some level of deep interpersonal connection (that is, *in-to-me-see)*. 'Intimacy' is sometimes used as a euphemism for sex, but this is reductive. Intimacy is also not a pre-requisite in sexual relationships; sex *can* involve and facilitate

* https://dictionary.cambridge.org/dictionary/english/intimacy

both intimacy and distance. In other words, sex can be used as a means of cultivating intimacy or protecting oneself against it.

It is a quality, and not an act. It can be found around a dinner table or a deathbed, on a sports pitch or video call. Fucking is no more or less intimate than doing up someone's tie, or sharing a dessert.

There can be intimacy, too, within restraint. If intimacy is a kind of deep knowing, a sense of understanding between two people, then it can be an act of knowing to stand aside, give someone space, if you know that is what they need. Intimacy is not confined to a specific place or type of person. It is an ongoing, co-created thing. It need not even be between two humans. Think of the meaningful, intimate communication one can have with a pet, or a sunset. Or, indeed, oneself.

The dictionary can only ever go so far in helping us to understand or describe the experience of intimacy. I asked people of different ages and orientations what they thought intimacy was. Interestingly, most people immediately jumped to describing intimacy as it exists within a sexual-romantic partnership. Not everyone, though. Here is a selection of what came back:

> **Susan:** 'Having left my marriage of twenty years – a marriage that was often very happy and fulfilling – to pursue a very intimate sexual and intellectual connection, I know intimacy takes many forms. Yes, it is about that kind of intense, passionate love-making that requires such deep trust and vulnerability, but it can also be the daily things that culminate over years – the living together as a household, arguing, snuggling, sulking and crying. Years of waking up next to each other with smelly breath. Parenting, cooking, taking the bins out – all that stuff.'

> **Michael:** 'I think affection and sexual intimacy is the key to a long-lasting, loving relationship. My husband and I show this to one another in small and large ways, though we do need reminding

at times. I also have some friends that I am very intimate with, in that we are very close and I trust them deeply, having relied on them during important life chapters.'

Rebecca: 'I think the key to intimacy is that you are pre-forgiven because you know that person enough to understand their baggage, and so you know there isn't malice in their behaviour and [you] don't hate them for it. My husband sometimes knows things about me that even I don't know about me . . . yet. He will have made an allowance for something I'm about to do before I know I'm even going to do it.'

Bryony: 'Intimacy is about lots of things, not just sex, but I think it's really important as a long-term couple to prioritise getting together naked. It might sound a bit cold or sterile but what I call "Nike sex" ("Just do it!") is vital for tuning in and feeling close to each other.'

Stine: 'It's like a quiet understanding of the other person. Whenever I think of intimacy, I get an image of my parents laughing at something and my mother putting her fingertips on my father's forearm – such a simple gesture and yet immensely intimate.'

Leng: 'Intimacy for me is less about sex than it has ever been, although of course that can be very intimate. It's more about someone wanting to hold my hand, or someone feeling proud of me for something. Also, if I can be small around someone [quiet, fragile] and know that they would hold me . . . That's intimacy.'

Moy: 'My partner and I have been together fifteen years, during which time my definition of intimacy has changed. Initially, it was about the physical intimacy and sex – the moments when I felt totally open and receptive to her touch or gaze. Now it's more about closeness, incidental touch – that hand on your shoulder that indicates support. It can be a look – like when I'm struggling and my partner just *knows* and offers a supportive smile. I suppose now I think of intimacy as a deep understanding of the other person, as well as a space in which one can be oneself, unedited, unfiltered and truly accepted. It's like a good wine – getting richer with age.'

The themes become apparent. Intimacy involves depth. It is a commitment to staying open-hearted and willing to communicate, to take on board your knowledge of another person and their history, and use that as a means to be closer to them and enhance trust. Interestingly, fewer people than I had expected mentioned words or having intimate conversations, but talked of being able to communicate without words. This resonated with me: one of the most intimate experiences of my life took place on my first day at therapy school, where each of us was instructed to stare in silence for five minutes into the eyes of another student and complete stranger. I will never forget that experience: excruciating, endless, extreme. At one point, I wanted to scream. At another, to sink. Then, for a while, I felt peaceful and then so exposed that I struggled not to run. Somehow, through pure grit, I made it to the end of the five minutes, though I was sweating. Afterwards, we were asked to feed back to our fellow eye-gazer on what we had noticed during the five minutes. Mine commented that she had found me fearful and quite guarded, describing in a nutshell those parts of myself I tended to hide in daily life, not just from others, but from myself. Here they were, exposed so clearly and silently, to a stranger in just five minutes.

Roadmarkers Towards Intimacy

Safety

As Dmitri's story indicates, we cannot be intimate if we don't feel safe enough to let our guard down. In order for him to be vulnerable and experience pleasure, Dmitri had to first develop trust that he wouldn't be judged for being himself. The best way he found of creating the conditions that could facilitate his exploration was to hire a professional, someone whose role was clear and where the boundaries were distinct.

For you, however, it may be different. Since we are all unique, each person has their own requirements of what they need to feel safe. This will likely change over time too. It will probably differ according to your connection and how much time you have already spent with that person.

A subjective sense of safety, however, is essential in order to achieve, or even conceive of, healthy intimacy. Even in the BDSM and kink communities, where pain or restraints are often experienced as pleasurable and erotic, these interactions usually involve strong ethical boundaries and very strict rules of engagement, like "safe words". Ask anyone in the world of BDSM, and they will tell you the dynamic is an incredibly intimate experience, facilitated by the underlying safety rules.

Safety starts within. For those who are lucky enough to have received solid parenting and not to have racked up any unresolved traumas, this internalised sense of safety may be familiar. For many others, it is something that can be built, sometimes over years, knowing that you are able to stand up for yourself and your needs where necessary. This may be controversial to some, who believe that intimacy can only be achieved with another person, but I believe that in adult relationships, achieving intimacy with another requires you to have a certain pre-existing level of intimacy-with-self: self-awareness and self-closeness. I know now that in taking care of and listening to myself, I am paving the way for intimacy with another. After all, it is difficult to engage in any kind of fulfilling, meaningful connection if I am unsure of my own boundary – where I end, and another begins. Having and giving enough space means there is a more distinctive *me,* with whom another can be intimate. Otherwise, we are enmeshed or disengaged.

The closeness we create together may either collapse into co-dependency, or else it burns off completely, much like water in the sun.

Vulnerability

Vulnerability is a key ingredient for building intimacy, since intimacy involves being more closely seen than in other relationship dynamics. Often, but not always, this means showing those aspects of ourselves that we tend to keep back, at least for a while. This can include the parts or characteristics that have been rejected by other people, or society, in the past.

Author and speaker Brené Brown is famous for her brilliant work on the beauty and importance of vulnerability. She defines it as 'uncertainty, risk and emotional exposure'. It is not weakness, she insists, but 'our most accurate measure of courage'.* Taking a risk in allowing someone else to see those aspects and accept them can be healing, as in Dmitri's story with the sexual surrogate, allowing us to move beyond past hurts and rework old, limiting narratives.

Does this mean that we can only be intimate with those who do not hurt our feelings – who *always* receive our truer selves with care? No, of course not, because a relationship of any depth that continues for long enough will experience issues. Whether large or small, this much is inevitable. To prepare ourselves for this inevitability is to automatically make ourselves vulnerable, because we cannot achieve intimacy without also opening ourselves up.

Human beings are mistake-making machines, however well-intentioned. What matters is what happens next. Have you ever had an argument with someone that led to a conversation to tackle a longstanding issue that was really upsetting you, and afterwards you felt closer than ever? If the answer is yes, then you have had a positive experience of what,

* Brown, B., *Daring Greatly: How the Courage to be Vulnerable Transforms the Way we Live, Love, Parent and Lead* (Penguin, 2013), p.34.

in therapy, is called 'rupture and repair'. Intimacy can feel compromised by the rupture, but it can amplify with repair.

Boundaries

In her book *The Dance of Intimacy,* psychotherapist Harriet Lerner defines an intimate relationship as 'one in which neither party silences, sacrifices or betrays the self and each party expresses strength and vulnerability in a balanced way'.*

When we come from a place of autonomy and self-compassion we can set appropriate boundaries and choose what to do next if/when they aren't met. Boundaries facilitate safety and thus allow for vulnerability. They show self-respect and allow the other person the important privilege of not having to read your mind. For one friend who's in a relationship with her married boyfriend, she requires at least twenty-four hours per week of quality time together. If that begins to fall away, there will be problems, and she has told him in no uncertain terms that she will not relent on this except in very exceptional circumstances. He has agreed quite happily to this but has a boundary of his own: there must be flexibility around which night of the week he sees her. Both know the score. As does his wife.

Roadblocks to Intimacy

'Roadblocks' are the word I use in therapy for anything that someone plonks in the middle of an interpersonal highway in order to stop progress down the road. 'Defences' is the word Sigmund Freud used, to refer to behaviours or thought processes people unconsciously use in order to avoid something that would otherwise be difficult to face.

* Lerner, H., *The Dance of Intimacy: A Woman's Guide to Courageous Acts of Change in Key Relationships* (Harper Perennial, 1990), p.3.

Digging into what might be your favourite roadblock in relationships is not about removing the use of roadblocks entirely, but about allowing you to notice what you are doing. It is only when we become conscious of a repetitive thought process or behaviour that we can ascertain whether it is, broadly speaking, good for us. There are occasions when they are necessary for safety. The problem comes when you have unknowingly put roadblocks all around and become stuck in one place. This is the opposite of choice. A kind of unconscious intimacy gridlock.

The roadblocks below are just a few examples of how we can avoid, or evade, intimacy. Getting to know your go-to roadblocks is an important step in the right direction when it comes to facilitating more choice about how, and with whom, you want to "do" intimacy in your life.

People-pleasing

Do you feel compelled to make others happy? Perhaps you avoid conflict or upsetting anyone, even at the expense of your wellbeing. People-pleasing is a big problem, particularly in British society where we tend to apologise when someone else steps on *our* foot! It is such a big and insidious problem, in fact, that we mistake it for politeness, or just for 'being a good egg'. But it is not a healthy trait, and it can lead to huge resentments, which rot your relationships from the inside out. Never has speaking your truth in the moment caused more damage than sitting on it for years. So why do people-pleasers not speak up? There are many reasons that originate from the simple desire to be liked. It poses a roadblock to intimacy as it avoids the challenge and vulnerability involved in having any real conflict (and the intimacy-enhancing opportunity for repair, referred to earlier, see page 72).

Busyness

Being excessively busy is one of the most insidious defences against intimacy that exists in society today. Work, for example, is often used as a way to avoid difficult conversations at home when things get strained, but we can keep ourselves too busy to deal with anything. When an activity or commitment is being used as a way of keeping a person or connection at arm's length, then it is a roadblock. And that's okay, sometimes, I think, provided you *know* you're doing it, because then, and only then, do you have a choice.

Distraction

You know that friend who thumbs through a magazine while chatting to you? Or the one who always turns up late and leaves early? One reason might be that they are fearful of intimacy, either consciously or unconsciously, because of the aforementioned risk of discomfort. The use of the mobile phone is the most obvious example of how people manage this type of anxiety, constantly scrolling or replying to messages. It ensures that we remain in contact with many, rather than in connection with just one. Social media is often used like a pacifier, I think: more like giving a baby a dummy than picking them up for a cuddle.

Deflection

Think of a light beam that gets deflected off a surface onto something else. Deflection is the art of turning the focus away from oneself and onto another person or subject. When taken to extremes, it can become a defence against vulnerability and closeness. Someone who continually deflects attention away from themselves, by answering a question with another question, or by keeping you talking about yourself, gets to keep themselves behind a shield.

Projection

Psychological projection is a classic, mostly unconscious roadblock, which can be used to prevent intimacy or anything that we do not wish to feel ourselves and so attribute to someone else. It is when someone feels so uncomfortable with something they are feeling or thinking that they push it onto the other person. A classic example is when someone says, *I feel like you're angry with me,* but it is them who feels angry with you. (I used to do that one, a lot.)

Drama/intensity

I once spoke to a wise older man about a relationship that I was struggling to leave, despite knowing, deep down, that I really needed to. I described the powerful connection I felt to my partner at the time, the intense passion we shared, second only to the incredible misery that we inflicted on each other. In truth, I could not understand why, given the mutual strong feelings, our relationship was not working. Especially when we shared such intimacy. When we were together, I explained, we were inseparable. When we were apart, we needed to be in contact several times a day; otherwise one or both of us got anxious. Leaving felt impossible; I needed the good parts of the relationship for my wellbeing. Yet the bad parts impacted on me so negatively I could barely see straight.

I was sure that I had never been closer to another person in my life, but I had to admit that I was unhappy living in a perpetual state of crisis.

'Sounds like you're mistaking intensity for intimacy,' he told me, direct and unapologetic.

'What?' I said.

I genuinely did not understand. What did he know about my relationship, anyway? How could he know what we had shared?

'Intimacy and intensity,' he repeated. 'They aren't the same.'

'What do you mean?' I asked, feeling my throat close up a little.

He went on to explain: intensity thrives off drama, whereas intimacy really does not. Intensity, however, can feel or appear like intimacy to those who grew up around emotional intensity, where the model/parental relationship at home was volatile, with extreme highs and lows.

Tick, tick . . . Ouch. Clearly, despite my professional knowledge and all the personal development work I had done, I had some serious blind spots here. As a therapist, I knew only too well how the relationships we witness as youngsters provide us with a blueprint for what is, or is not, appropriate or desirable. Even if we watched in horror and promised ourselves that we would never enter a relationship, as adults, like theirs, the chances are that on some level we will end up repeating it at least once. Either that or we will ensure we have the polar opposite dynamic, which can be just as limiting.

In all the intensity of my former relationship, I had sacrificed and betrayed myself a great deal. I suspect, also, that my partner had sacrificed themselves too, albeit in different ways that only they will really know. After all, you can't keep a dysfunctional dynamic alive on your own. We had co-created an intensity borne out of fear rather than trust, and our intimacy had suffered.

Intimacy, instead, is facilitated by some separateness, a quota of space between two people. It is not about merging entirely with another person, or a process of 'enmeshment', where personal boundaries are unclear and people take on other people's emotions. Nor is it about disengagement, where boundaries are overly rigid. In other words, it is not about co-dependence or anti-dependence, but about inter-dependence: being able to feel connected to another and maintaining one's own identity. If we cannot allow ourselves the necessary space required to develop and maintain autonomy, then how can we truly show ourselves to another?

I have learnt, through trial and error, that intimacy grows with kindness, not with demand or distance. Healthy intimacy between people is a necessarily co-created process, as is its opposite: dysfunction. We must observe as much as we act; we must stay quiet as much as we speak. When done consciously and mindfully, developing a sense of intimacy is a privilege and to be honoured.

This is rarely a linear or straightforward process: layers that have been sharply peeled away can also be re-adopted just as sharply. We can fall in and out of intimacy, just as we can fall in and out of romantic love. When we show ourselves to another in this moment, we are not just being courageous, but also risking rejection and loss. It is a fragile state, but it can be healing. This beautiful process is full of responsibility. As such, we should be discerning about who we choose to co-create such intimacy with so as to avoid unnecessary destruction. *Who do you want to give your heart to? What qualities should they have? What can you give, what can you take? What can you compromise and collaborate on?* And, most crucially, *What can you forgive?*

It is harder to go back and save our hearts than to go forward and offer them. I don't think my twenty-year-old self, with her idealistic view of love, would ever have understood this. Nor would I have accepted that developing deep physical and emotional closeness with someone is as much about respecting their autonomy as it is about becoming entwined. At thirty I might have understood it, cognitively, but could not yet live it. My forty-year-old self can do both now. She also respects that we all have differing levels of emotional availability according to our nature. The only way to grow as individuals, then, is by not seeking to change or blame the other, but to inquire into and own our emotional needs.

Choice and Intimacy – In Essence

The dictionary definition of intimacy only goes so far in describing it. Our perception of intimacy can be fluid, rather than fixed. As our perspective on relationships changes, so too can our perspective on what intimacy is. Yet it is always – virtually without exception – a context-driven and subjective experience. There can be no real intimacy without safety, vulnerability or autonomy. The more you are in contact with yourself – your sensations, emotions, thoughts, desires, etc. – the more you can stay intimate with others. We also need boundaries – to know where one person begins, and another person ends – in order to really be intimate.

In order to protect ourselves from vulnerability, and from being intimate with others, there are certain 'roadblocks' we use. Sometimes these are consciously used, and sometimes unconsciously used. They include people-pleasing, busyness, distraction, projection and drama. Intimacy can be mistaken for intensity because we often have intense relationships with those we feel emotionally entwined with. Perpetual volatility within a relationship is *not* the same as sustainable intimacy. One feeds off drama, the other respect. Yes, both can involve passion, but where intimacy allows for boundaries, intensity will blaze right through them.

Choice and Intimacy – Inquiry

Your intimacy blueprint

What does intimacy mean to you? How does it relate to words like 'closeness' or 'connection'? When you think of being intimate with someone, what comes to mind? What do you love or hate when it comes to intimacy?

Take some time to think about and question your ideas around affection, tenderness, communication, silence, privacy, connection. What have you absorbed from society? What have you observed in the behaviour of those around you, regarding boundaries and taking space? Where, or with whom, do you feel most totally yourself?

Other useful questions you might ask yourself include:

- How much of yourself do you feel you have to deprioritise in order to maintain a connection with another? Apply this to someone you are intimate with.
- In what ways would you like to work on your ability to be intimate? What would be a good first step? Can you take it now? If not, why not? Look honestly at your blocks, your resentments and your fear.
- Think about what you need to feel safe enough to let your guard down. Perhaps also note what it means, for you, to feel unsafe/not

safe enough to achieve intimacy. One obvious example would be that we need to not feel under threat, or at risk of harm.

- Next, think about the most memorable moments in your life that have been associated with a sense of intimacy, and how comfortable you felt in those moments to speak your truth. What did you do immediately after? What do you feel when you remember? How does thinking about intimacy shed light on your current or past relationships, romantic or not? Think about how much space you are allowed. And how much closeness you allow yourself. What is 'normal' to you? What is abnormal, or too much?
- You might also consider how your definition of intimacy has changed over time. I used to regard it as primarily being about romantic connection. Now I prioritise it across all my relationships, including with myself. There may be key ingredients required to achieve intimacy, but those flavours of intimacy can differ.

Your intimacy roadblocks

Think for a moment: how do *you* duck out of tricky conversations, or manage your own uncomfortable feelings when those difficult moments crop up? Some people are blatant: they just ignore a situation in the hope that eventually it will go away. I had one client who always began to yawn whenever we touched on something important, and another who immediately seemed to need the toilet. Others described dashing to the gym at the first sign that a deeper level of connection was going to be required of them. Some turn to drugs, the bookies or the biscuit tin. It is not the actions or behaviours themselves that are a problem, but the reasons for doing them – which, in this case, was to shift discomfort rather than explore it.

Pay attention, also, to *when* you set down a roadblock. Do you have the urge to start making a smoothie, noisily, just when your lover puts their arms around you? Yes, you could be craving a smoothie, but really: *right* now? Perhaps you stay up late, long after your partner has gone to bed, and play guitar until 2 a.m. There is nothing necessarily wrong with that, of course, unless you are doing it to avoid whatever intimate activity bedtime brings. If you really cannot think of anything you do in this vein, then ask someone close to you. Chances are you'll be surprised at what they have noticed in your behaviour.

The next question to ask yourself is, of course: do I really want to keep doing this? The answer *no* is the first step to affecting change but hardly the only one. Actually changing is a lot harder than deciding to change, and here you'll need a whole lot of self-compassion and patience. It's practice that makes progress (not perfect, because that's impossible) and progress usually involves moving generally forward in a fairly haphazard way. That's not only normal but reassuring. Remember the story of 'The Tortoise and the Hare'? When I forget it, I'm in trouble.

When I did this exercise, I had the massive insight that I use talking as a roadblock. If there is an awkward silence or something strange has happened in a conversation, I will often start to chatter. I literally fill the painful space that has opened between us with the sound of my own voice. The silence feels too intimate. It might betray my feelings, and that is too risky – I will be "seen" – a vulnerability too far when I'm already feeling rejected or misunderstood. Now that I know this about myself, I am actively working on staying with awkward silences for as long as possible before I chatter or apologise. This allows me to stay tuned in to my feelings, or to give the other person a chance to speak first. Very often, we turn a corner. My chatter can act just like a roadblock, but now that I'm aware of that, I have options. *To block or not to block. It is my choice, and I can question.*

Now What?

You've considered how intimacy shows up in your life, including the ways you encourage it or push it away. You might now be feeling a bit fragile. Perhaps even overexposed. Some of what's written in this chapter might have challenged your idea of what intimacy actually is, too, and how it relates to taking space. There is no need to do anything specific now. Raising self-awareness in this way can, in and of itself, instigate change.

CHAPTER 4

CHOICE AND SEX

A Sex Life Less Ordinary – *Sandy and Jon's Story**

'I don't worry that my girlfriend is about to run away with everyone she has an attraction to, dates or sleeps with! I mean, if you trust someone enough to go out with them then you trust them enough to make good decisions.' (Jon)

Sandy and Jon are North Londoners in their late forties. In many ways, they are a conventional long-term couple. They have been together eleven years and share a mortgage, a car and a cat. In other ways, though, they are not so conventional: both are bisexual and have no interest in monogamy. Sometimes stuff just . . . *happens* and that's okay. One-night stands or a flirtation? It adds some colour and sparkle to life. Why would they deny each other that? They want security *and* adventure. So they've decided to have both.

It hasn't always been straightforward. Jon was in a monogamous relationship when they hooked up and Sandy was married to another member of the large friendship group that they went out with every weekend.

By their own admission, both of their relationships were doomed. But still, Sandy admits, 'The way Jon and I got together certainly wasn't ethical. We should have broken up with our partners first. Instead, we got found out – hotel receipts left in my pocket, intimate emails found by his girlfriend; that kind of thing. People got hurt. We handled it badly. It was awful.'

First, Jon broke up with his girlfriend. A few months later, Sandy's marriage ended. The wider friendship group were furious and ostracised the cheating pair, which meant that for a while Sandy and Jon were one another's main drinking buddy. It was clear, during one of many long and intimate Saturday nights spent out for dinner or in the pub, that their old friendship circle had been full of unconscious rules they did not believe in and they both had a sexually adventurous streak, which, until now, they had kept secret. Sandy told Jon that she and her ex had attended some upmarket swingers' parties. These had been fun but a little pretentious, she explained, as well as limited by her husband's insistence that she refrain from any physical contact with other men – instead, touching only other women, and when he was watching (sigh).

Jon was less amused than unimpressed. He would never restrict Sandy in this way, he promised, not only because it was just 'a total arsehole move' but because he understood the desire to explore other bodies and connections. It was something he, too, had investigated, using the internet to find couples he fancied and then, if there was rapport, to meet for sex.

Sandy was intrigued by this. The conversation unlocked something, and they decided to pool their resources to explore the world of play parties, sexy websites and dating apps together. There followed a very eye-opening and exuberant few years of exploration, the best of which involved attending monthly invite-only community gatherings. These 'kinky salons', as they were known, focused primarily on self-expression, creativity and playfulness, alongside sex. It was more like a carnival than a soirée, attended by guests of every conceivable style, identification and body type – nothing like the parties she'd been to with her ex, where everyone was very beautiful and polished. Here, you couldn't just show up;

existing members could bring someone new, but they had to look after that person. The idea was to make sure nobody felt threatened. Everyone was divided into groups of eight and given a talk by the host about consent and communication.

The party was always staged, with bars and novelty photo booths open from the start, along with optional sexy activities like rope bondage or tantra. At around eleven o'clock there would be a performance – cabaret or burlesque – and then the DJ would arrive and crank up the music. At that time the "playrooms" would open up around the sides of the dance floor. Each one had a massive bin full of free condoms, lube and dental dams, but other than that the exact layout differed; there was usually a main playroom with beds and fluffy pillows, and other, smaller rooms with BDSM furniture for other, kinkier activities. Everyone felt catered for.

Exploring this underground world was not something they could forget. Here, they met people who shared some of their primary values around the freedom to experience new things. It was like a door had been flung open to a new, exciting way of life and they had no desire to close it.

One opportunity led to another, Sandy reveals. 'The parties were a gateway, I guess. Once, we started chatting to a couple as we left one of the kinky salons and ended up taking them home with us and having sex for the rest of the night! We also met people there who we got on with, and we developed a circle of sex friends that extended beyond the parties. Instead of being invited to someone's for dinner, you'd be invited for dinner and shagging. It all brought me and Jon closer, really, like this shared naughty secret that we could giggle about for weeks after.'

As they got older and progressed in their respective careers, Sandy and Jon began to work harder and party less. When they did have the occasional sexy evening out it would invariably leave them horny and excitable, revving up the passion at home. It was still something they only did in the presence of the other, although that changed, quite suddenly, five years into their relationship.

'One of the friends who we sometimes had sex with wanted to go out with us for dinner on his birthday, and I explained that I was away on business but said to Sandy that she should still go and maybe spend the evening with him. I didn't think she was about to run away with him, but I knew she liked him. She's a flirtatious, social creature and I didn't want to stop that aspect of her life. I guess I felt like opportunities were going to arise when I am not there, and I don't want to stop her living her best life.'

Initially, Sandy was reluctant about what seemed like a strange step. Going home with someone else *without* Jon there felt risky, like it might threaten their happy state, so she agreed to meet their friend for dinner only. As the evening progressed and the wine flowed, however, she relaxed. Meanwhile, her phone was buzzing. It was Jon. He was reminding her that he was okay with the thought of her and their friend having sex. Not just okay, in fact: turned on. *I think you should go for it,* he wrote. *Have an amazing, sexy night. I'd really love to hear about it . . . x*

You can probably guess what happened next.

After that, the rules shifted. Very quickly, it became normal for either Sandy or Jon to be physical with someone without the other being present. They always told each other and never missed a sexy detail. The fun they had outside of their relationship had become an integral, and positive, part of it.

It's not compulsory, though, says Sandy: 'If a year passes and neither of us goes on a date or has sex with someone else, just because we are busy or content, then that's fine! It's just like if months and months pass and you haven't gone to the cinema or whatever – it's something you enjoy, and want to do again, but haven't got around to because you've had other stuff going on.'

This is something I hear a lot from non-monogamous folk: that sex can be viewed like any other activity and not something that must be done *together.* It takes a shift of perspective to get here for most of us. So how have Sandy and Jon achieved such freedom? And is there really no jealousy *at all*? If we have grown up around the typical monogamous blueprint, it seems bizarre. Beyond the blueprint, however, it happens. Sandy and Jon are living proof.

Jon says: 'I feel like there's an unwritten rule people adopt in traditional relationships, a kind of ownership, like it's all right to say, *No, you can't go out with them*, or, *No, you can't go and meet your ex.* But I don't own Sandy; she is continuing to be herself, and just because she's going out with me doesn't mean she shouldn't do what the hell she wants.'

Does Sandy feel the same vis-à-vis Jon?

'Absolutely. I don't want Jon to feel like he shouldn't make eye contact with someone on the Tube in case it leads somewhere illicit! Both of us really value that spark when you meet someone for the first time. It's such a lovely part of being human. It doesn't mean you want to marry that person, just that you have a connection. I want us both to be able to explore that when it arises, whether that ends up being a drink and/or sex!'

Like most of those in the consciously non-monogamous community, both Sandy and Jon take their sexual health, and the health of others, very seriously, so unsafe sex is a no-go. Although there is nothing else explicitly banned from their arrangement, Jon is not interested in having multiple deep and committed romantic attachments, and nor is Sandy.

'I once dated a really cool guy who shared a lot of my interests and tastes. He knew the set-up, but after a while he started saying and doing things that made it clear he wanted a more boyfriend/girlfriend style commitment,' Sandy added. 'I started to feel really uncomfortable – I couldn't give him what he wanted and had to end it pretty quickly, explaining that I only wanted one long-term boyfriend and that position was already taken. This isn't polyamory.'

Open, but with limits. The message is clear and consistent. But what if they had never been open, I wonder? It may not be a freedom that they need to act on regularly, but if sex with other people was completely out of bounds, would Sandy and Jon still be together?

Sandy hesitates, looks at Jon, who laughs, and then: 'I think one or both of us would have accidentally slept with someone else and that would have combusted the whole thing, unnecessarily.'

'At least this way we don't have to worry about sex breaking us up,' Jon agrees.

This is an interesting idea, and one I have heard before from open couples: the notion that the more relaxed we might be about exclusivity, the less our bonds can be threatened. It also reminds me of the Buddhist concept of non-attachment and a particular analogy from author Martine Batchelor, about holding an object made of gold. If we know something is precious, then we are tempted to grip onto it very tightly. But what arrives then is just pain: our arm and hand cramp under the tension. But we should not drop the object either, says Batchelor, because that would be just as destructive. Rather, we must hold it lightly with our palm open, so we can put it down and pick it up, and use our hand for something else.*

Sandy and Jon demonstrate, I think, how at its best an open relationship can offer effective inoculation against the devastation of cheating, the trust-demolishing properties of which can wreck relationships, fast. At its *very* best, it can go beyond inoculation and even strengthen the existing bond, by facilitating a deeper tried-and-tested trust. For them, their loyalty is built upon things other than sexual exclusivity. They need not limit each other's bodies in order to be chosen. There is a genuine buoyancy to the way this couple discuss sex and non-monogamy – a quality that I have scarcely witnessed.

Before I met them, I had begun to wonder if a high level of heartache and anguish was just part of the deal; one gets to have more sexual freedom in return for having to face jealousy head-on. You might think that if something causes so much trouble, it must be unnatural – at odds with the way we 'ought' to be, as humans. I might have pushed this

* Paraphrased from Batchelor, M., *Meditation for Life* (London: Frances Lincoln, 2001).

argument myself a few years ago, but I've spoken to enough people with different lifestyles to truly believe that there are myriad ways to 'do' relationships and it's not up to me to judge. But what about how our brains are wired? I interviewed anthropologist and human behaviour researcher Helen Fisher, who has been outspoken on this topic, referring to CNM as 'transparent adultery'. Fisher bemoaned the 'enormous amount of time these people spend discussing their feelings, because it's really not natural. Throughout history there have been free-love communes, but the bottom line is that we aren't built for this, even in societies where it is the tradition.'

Fisher's reasoning is not without a scientific basis. Having extensively studied the brain systems involved in lust and attachment, she concludes that where romantic love is present, so too is sexual possessiveness: 'When you begin to fall in love, you really care if they are sleeping with other people. Along with the evolution of pair bonding, we also evolved a host of other brain systems to support this drive, and one of them is jealousy. We are a jealous animal. Even in societies that absolutely permit polygyny [multiple wives], the wives try to kill the other wives' children by poisoning them.'*

Sandy and Jon's story doesn't exactly fit Fisher's conclusive declarations about jealousy and monogamy. They, and the similar people I've met, suggest that however compelling the brain science, one size does not, *ever*, fit all. Certainly, this couple have been together long enough to be very familiar to each other. But they were sexually non-exclusive form the get-go and seem to still be in love with one another. As for jealousy, there really isn't any. No storm clouds, nor extreme winds. It is, for the most part, sunny. I still have no clear answer on *how* exactly they have managed this; perhaps it is the fact that both Sandy and Jon have similar levels of extraversion and confidence and have few sexual hang-ups. Perhaps it's this, combined with the fact that their childhoods were jealousy-free and provided them with good-enough parenting of the

* Interview with Helen Fisher, anthropologist and author of *Anatomy of Love: A Natural History of Mating, Marriage and Why We Stray*, October 2020.

type that creates secure-enough adults. Perhaps it is also a whole host of other factors that only they, together, will understand.

Whatever the magic recipe is for their success, the honesty and openness that they have achieved is quite astonishing, particularly when one considers the unethical way they got together. Their shared values and outlooks are crucial, I think, with neither of them adopting the age-old romantic, monogamous idea that one person can answer all of another's needs and wants, both in the bedroom *and* intellectually *and* emotionally *and* spiritually *and* . . . everything.

Sandy concludes: 'Trust means that this person loves you and has your best interests at heart. And for us, trust does not mean we can't shag someone else. I know that Jon can have an incredible night with another woman, or a man, and it doesn't have any impact on how he feels about me. I know this because I've experienced the same thing. The idea that lust is finite just seems so odd! Like there won't be any left for my partner just because I allow myself to express lust for someone else.'

The Sexual Blueprint

Before we start considering any individual's blueprint when it comes to sex, let's question *what sex is.* Where does it start? Where does it end? Taking someone's phone number can be sexual. As can the way someone walks. What about eye contact? When is it flirting or 'just banter'? And at what point are you definitely 'having sex'? Is there *always* a clear difference?

I know many, mostly heterosexual, people who think that sex always involves penetration. Some think it must also involve orgasm – the male orgasm, at least. The dictionary definition states that sex = sexual intercourse = the act of having sex, especially sex between a man and a woman, in which the man puts his penis inside the woman's vagina.*

* https://www.macmillandictionary.com/dictionary/british/sexual-intercourse

Especially? This is what I mean by *blueprint*: where we hold one ideal above another. Here, the form of intercourse that is deemed to most equate to 'real sex' is the heterosexual kind, and one particular act – the act that can culminate in pregnancy – is elevated over any other. Even the Wikipedia entry for sexual intercourse shows this bias, where sex is defined as '*typically* involving the insertion and thrusting of a penis into a vagina' though it does add 'for sexual pleasure, reproduction or both'. Further down it is acknowledged that 'sex can mean any form of sexual activity'. That's great. But still. It's obvious that most people grow up with a clear hierarchy around what definitely constitutes sex and what might not.

Of course, there are historical and evolutionary arguments for why sex is still defined first and foremost as a heterosexual penetrative act. But in the 2020s can we be more fluid (pun intended) and allow ourselves a little subjectivity and nuance? What is sex for you? Beyond the official definition, I mean. Is it 'real' sex if you are alone, or is it 'just' masturbation? Is it sex if no one comes? Does it count if you're blind drunk? I don't believe there are right answers here, just information to be gleaned, ideas and thoughts to make us more conscious.

Dictionary definition aside, so much of sex is subjective. At times, I have even wondered if sex might be closer to a state of being than an act of doing; a physical or metaphysical space one inhabits, rather than something one does, gives, takes, thinks or feels. For many of us, language is important. Does "having sex" mean something different from "fucking"? And what about "making love"? Despite being a grown-up in all other areas, I still cringe like an immature teen upon hearing these two words, which conjure up images of earnest caressing of the skin before moving, slowly and in sepia, into the missionary position. Developing an awareness of your own personal meta-dictionary (the spin you add to certain terms) can be useful in becoming more conscious around yourself and sex. Why do so many people use words like 'nailing', 'boning', 'smashing' and 'pounding' for having sex with someone – is there something erotic about aggression or is it all just about patriarchy?

My sexual blueprint – an example

In the inquiry section of this chapter, you'll be encouraged to think about your own sexual blueprint: the messages you absorbed growing up and how you think about, and approach, sex today. It's a helpful exercise, and one I've done myself, so I thought I'd offer my own sexual blueprint as an example.

As a young, heterosexual woman, my views on sex were in line with most dictionary definitions, in that I didn't consider kissing, getting naked or even oral sex to be "real" sex. If it didn't involve actual penetration with a penis then it was just "fooling around" and did not merit an official notch on my bedpost. At this stage in my life, keeping the notch numbers down really mattered because of the blueprint I had grown up with, including Catholicism and the wider cultural messages fed to women about what they should and should not do in order to be a worthwhile female human. Promiscuity was a sin. Promiscuity, by the way, meant having sex with *anyone* whom I did not love. I knew I did not want to be 'the kind of person who had sex with lots of people', but I also felt compelled, socially and physically, to sexually mature. These 'not-real-sex' encounters meant I could explore physically with someone without having to experience guilt, shame or risk, or re-evaluate my self-image.

Though I did not question it until I was much older, I had come to understand that enjoying sex was okay as a heterosexual woman, just so long as I was in a committed, loving relationship. This, I had also learnt, was never more important than when it came to a woman's first sexual experience, which must not happen too early or without thought. Pleasure was not something I heard much about, nor was desire. In fact, I remember getting the distinct impression that to be sexually desirous was wanton, and would lead me, as a female, into trouble. Men, however, could do what they wanted, *and they would* (so watch out)! The same rules did not apply to them. Unlike women, they weren't weak or amoral for being lusty. They were just doing what men did. It was up to women to withstand it and keep their legs closed unless they were loved and/or married.

In my early twenties, I had moved out of home and spent time at university mixing with different people who were more outspoken than me about desire and sex, and I relaxed my views. By this point, I had even found some enjoyment in sex with men – one in particular – though hypervigilance lingered around how I should appear, behave or move. I will never forget the mixture of shame and confusion I felt when my older, more sexually experienced boyfriend looked down at me during sex and said, 'Could you try to look less stoic?' I knew immediately what he meant, but that was impossible when I was so self-conscious and disconnected from my body. There were moments when I felt turned on, but mostly I was physically numbed, all subtler sensations drowned out by anxious and self-critical thoughts. On the whole, sex was guilt-ridden and complicated. It was something I preferred to do when drunk, the alcohol shushing my anxious mind so that my body could wilt and wander.

But I had sex with a woman for the first time in my mid-twenties. This was a transformative experience and also one that entirely threatened my blueprint about what sex was and how much I should enjoy it. Given that women can have sex without any kind of paraphernalia that resembles a penis, I no longer knew what constituted 'real sex' and had to re-evaluate my ideas on just how many people I had slept with. What she and I were doing certainly *was* sex, I decided, since it involved nakedness, exploration, pleasure, intimacy, orgasm, bodily fluids and a whole heap of other ingredients that I thought more significant than just having a penis inside me. My ideas continued to shift, and at thirty-five I met another lover, with whom I had new experiences that have become an integral part of my ideas on sex and sexuality, and helped me to add more depth and colour to my sex blueprint than I ever dreamt possible. In essence, I have traced over my blueprint many times and will, I hope, continue to add layers to it as time goes on.

Thinking Outside the Sex Blueprint: Sexual Identity, Preference and Language

With more awareness comes more choice, but sometimes we need knowledge too. For Sandy and Jon, it was attending various sex parties that gave them fuller access to a whole new world of being in relationships. Here, they met people who were kinky, non-binary, polyamorous, non-monogamous, transgender, and pansexual.

As a therapist, I am cautious of labelling, for fear that it might limit a person's self-image and hinder positive change. When it comes to choice, however, knowing the labels can be important. How can we know what our choices are if we don't have a word for them? Think about the term 'non-binary', which, in terms of gender, is used to refer to someone who chooses not to identify with an exclusively male or female gender. Without that term, such people still existed, but having a word that offers some explanation as to where they stand in terms of gender identity allows them to be seen and heard in everyday conversations.

As such, this section focuses on pulling out of the woodwork some of the less 'blueprinty' forms of sexual identities or styles. I don't intend, nor am I able, to cover all the different sexual identities or practices here. As with the brief descriptions of various types of non-monogamy in Chapter Two (see page 47), this is not an exhaustive list but a chance to get clear on some of the ways people describe their sexuality in the choice-ist world of conscious sexuality.

Sexual attraction and identity – some important terms

<u>Asexual:</u> A sexual orientation that refers to someone who doesn't experience sexual attraction or sexual desire. They may experience mental and emotional attraction.

<u>Allosexual:</u> The word for someone who does experience sexual attraction, although since asexuality is so far removed from the blueprint, we rarely need to use a word to denote its alternative.

Alosexual: Someone who has no physical or mental attraction to any specific gender, or usually any other person, though (unlike asexual people) they do enjoy sexual pleasure, mostly alone.

Intersex: Previously referred to as hermaphrodites. A person who is born with variations in sex characteristics.

Demisexual: A sexual orientation referring to people who are only sexually attracted to people after they feel a strong emotional connection. This is not the same as choosing to have sex with people once you already feel close to them emotionally; it means someone who does not feel *any* attraction to anyone in any situation unless they are already bonded with that person.

Pansexual: Capable of sexual and romantic attraction to people regardless of their gender identity or sex. This does not mean you are attracted to everyone, merely that your preferences are, a bit, well . . . panoramic.

Sex positive: An explicit statement about an attitude to sex that brings a total lack of negative judgement. In her book *Sex Positive*, social psychologist Dr Kelly Neff writes: 'The sex positive movement is a philosophical movement that promotes and embraces sexuality and sexual expression, with an emphasis on safe and consensual sex. Sex positive relationships are ones where partners support each other's choices and decisions without judgement, guilt or slut shaming.'*

Kink: The spectrum of the more unusual sexual practices, which are not as uncommon as you might think. A person might be called 'kinky' for enjoying consensual sexual relationships involving roleplay or fantasy.

* Neff, Dr K., *Sex Positive: Redefining Our Attitudes to Love and Sex* (Watkins, 2020), p.9.

BDSM: The world of kink can include BDSM but doesn't have to. BDSM refers to various erotic practices or behaviours involving bondage, discipline, dominance, submission, sadism, masochism . . . Consent is very important in the BDSM world. The term can also be used to describe relationships and communities and tends to include power play and/or roles and roleplay. It contains its own subcultures and rules of engagement.

What Does (Having More) Choice Within Sex Look Like?

If we are talking about conscious choice, then we should talk about conscious sex. This term has connotations of spirituality, kink, tantra, non-monogamy and pretentiousness! It need not be so complicated: becoming more conscious in one's sexual life and sexuality is just one aspect of becoming more conscious generally, i.e. a person who is present in the moment, aware and mindful of oneself and one's surroundings. In essence, conscious sexuality is about practising presence and self-awareness during sex and all things sexual. We might talk about being alive to the flow of energy between yourself and your sexual partner(s). Or we might just say *not* being on autopilot. One thing's for sure: it is on a spectrum, rather than the binary *either* conscious *or* unconscious.

If expanding choice results partly from expanding and enhancing self-awareness, then it is important to take note of what goes on inside your mind. I still remember the day that a lover first asked me what sexual fantasies I had and how difficult I found it to answer the question. It was not just that I was bashful about responding, but I had rarely thought about the question. I was surprised, and actually quite sad, to realise that, thanks to the stringent sexual blueprint I'd grown up with, I had not allowed myself an erotic mental playground.

I was oblivious to the way I had limited my own freedoms until somebody asked the question and a door opened to an empty room. Slowly, through a process of mental and physical exploration, I started to uncover some of my fantasies. I am now a huge advocate of people paying attention to their fantasies and turning towards their internal world. As with the earlier investigation into your sexual blueprint (see page 90), this requires an element of courage, particularly if you have a strong sense of the blueprint in terms of sexual desire. It might be hard, I know, but try to maintain a curious and open-minded – rather than judgemental – stance here. The fastest way to kill creativity and personal exploration is self-criticism and the introduction of rules. Taking note of our inner landscapes can help unravel some 'blueprint-itis' and lead to a more authentic and fulfilling relationship with sex, *whatever that means for you.*

Choice and Consent – An Important Note

Without consent, we have no choice. That much, I think, is obvious. What is less clear-cut is the question of what constitutes consent and what enables conscious consent. At its most obvious, sexual consent is about agreeing or refusing to do something, and being physically able to make that clear. We know, for example, that it is a crime to force someone to have sex when they are explicitly stating they don't want to. But what about being emotionally able to speak up? What if a person's fear of rejection or upsetting a partner propels them into agreeing to keep going with a situation that they don't want?

'Being able to agree to something requires everyone involved feeling free enough and safe enough to tune into ourselves, and to communicate openly with others, about who we are, what our capacities are, and what we want and don't want,' writes the academic and author M-J Barker, who has tackled consent quite extensively in their work.*

* https://www.rewriting-the-rules.com/consent-work/

Consent can be nuanced and complex, especially where intense and/or historic relational dynamics are at play. It is often an ongoing process rather than a singular decision. At every stage possible, there should be choice. Part of this 'being able to agree to something' involves being informed enough about what that something is that you can consciously consent. Arguably, one can't consent to something the consequences or process of which they do not fully understand.

There are all sorts of ways in which we negate the importance of real consent. There are also lots of ways in which we can pressure a person into doing something they don't want to do. It can be subtle, or even unconscious, and yet it happens everywhere. I do not believe that any one of us has *never* in our lives manipulated someone else into doing something. There are also some occasions when it might be necessary to ignore or refuse consent, like when my toddler is hitting me in the face. I don't ask for his consent to take his arm and pull it away from my cheek – I just do it. When I'm tickling him, however, I keep asking for his consent, even when he is still laughing. 'Do you want Mummy to keep on tickling?' I say. Very often he says no. Then, a minute later, he says yes. We begin again, and I ask again. Just because he wanted tickling thirty seconds ago, doesn't mean he cannot change his mind.

I am not suggesting you check with your sexual partner every thirty seconds whether they want you to continue. (I mean, you *could* and it's called 'enthusiastic consent'). What is important to note, however, is that certain assumed markers of consent – or in this case, arousal – may not always equate. Sex expert and writer Emily Nagoski covers this in her important book *Come As You Are* when she delves into the idea of arousal non-concordance. This is when a person's genital response does not match their reported levels of felt arousal. The genitals tell you what is sexually relevant, she insists, but only the person can tell you whether they are turned on. Next, Nagoski cites research and states that there is approximately a 50 per cent overlap between what a male's genitals respond to as sexually relevant and sexually appealing and just a 10 per cent overlap in these two in a female.* To put this more bluntly: just because a woman's genitals are wet, does not necessarily mean she is keen to have sex, and, similarly, if she is not wet, it does not mean she isn't aroused. Also, just because a man has an erection, does not necessarily indicate he consents to sex. It may sound boring or plain unsexy, but making sure somebody really wants something is the gateway to consensual, respectful sex. And *that,* of course, is sexy.

'In order to consent to something, we have to fully and profoundly know that we don't have to do that thing, now or ever,' writes Barker. 'This applies whether the thing in question is having sex with a partner, doing the task we'd set ourselves on a particular day, hanging out with a friend or being in a certain relationship or group. We have to know that nothing is contingent on it, that we're not bound by entitlement or obligation, that there'll be no punishment if we don't do it, and that there's no assumed default "normal" script or path that we're expected to follow.'

I like M-J Barker's consent criteria, not only because it demonstrates how frighteningly easy it is to unconsciously *not* consent, to be coerced or emotionally blackmailed into something, but because it also reminds us of why choice matters: that without consent there is no choice, and without choice there is no consent.

Choice and Sex – In Essence

Nobody can truly enjoy more choice around sex/their sexuality if they are besieged by shame, body hatred, self-consciousness, guilt and anxiety. If you struggle with any of these things then taking time to gently explore your feelings, ideally with a trained professional, is the least that you deserve.

* Nagoski, E., *Come As You Are: The Surprising New Science That Will Transform Your Sex Life* (Scribe, 2015).

Without consent, we can't have choice, and without choice, we can't consent. But what does *consent* really mean? Consent is complex and multivalent. It is also a prerequisite to conscious choice, so it's worth exploring what consent means to *you*. Taking more conscious ownership of your sexuality and sexual choices is all good, but this isn't just about having more/better sex. It also involves taking sexual health seriously, getting regularly checked and taking precautions where necessary.

Choice and Sex – Inquiry

Have you got a clear idea of your sexual blueprint? The kind of ideas and rules you grew up with in regard to sex and sexuality? What did you absorb from external sources? What lessons did the media feed you and how did this, and your view of sex and sexuality, change as time went on?

Next, think about the most memorable moments in your life that have been associated with sex – the highs and the lows. How do they speak of your concerns? What are your current beliefs around sex, particularly around what you are or are *not* allowed to want or explore? This might include a long, wordy description or it could be a few lines, a diagram or a sketch. If you have an inkling as to where these beliefs originated, write that down too.

Concentrate specifically on any obvious judgements that come up, either about yourself or other people. Who are you now, sexually, and do you feel you have full choice? Who might you like to be – or become – if you were free of fear or rules? Try not to censor yourself here – this can be a totally private document where you can tell yourself the truth. This is about raising self-awareness, not self-consciousness. Only once you get clear on your blueprint can you begin to trace over it with new ideas.

Have you ever had sex, or continued with sex, just because you thought you should? What is the thing you would never tell anyone about you and sex? What would you want them very much to know? What value do you place on consent in sex and relationships – both yours and another's – and how might you have respected or disrespected consent in the past?

Have there been any times when your guilt and/or shame have got in the way of you exploring sex and your sexuality? What were the messages running around your head?

Were there any times when you have successfully gone beyond any limiting aspects of your sexual blueprint in order to bring more adventure into your life?

Is there anything you would really love to do, or try, in sex, that you don't feel you are allowed to do?

Do you regard sex as a means of connection, or an expression of connection? Both can be valid approaches, and they can change with different people.

Now that you have uncovered some of the things you think about sex, take a closer look. Does that blueprint still work for you? Just for a moment, set aside any inherited rules you have around sex. What could you add/take away, to reflect who you are right now?

How would you really like your sex life to look? Stop worrying about what anyone else might think – remember, this is a private inquiry – and be honest with yourself about your ideal sexual relationship(s). Next, imagine that you tell your partner(s) what you really desire and they don't want all the same things. What can you, or can't you, compromise on?

Now What?

Hopefully you answered those questions without self-censoring; you've got a clearer view of your inherited ideas about sex and have begun to see where there's room for growth and exploration. Maybe you're already planning a night out in the local sex club or investing in some new and kinky sex toys. You might, however, not be so jubilant. Sex is a complex topic and one that commonly brings up great swathes of toxic shame, so please be gentle with yourself and consider seeking help from a qualified professional if shame is a regular visitor in your life. We'll look more at shame in the next few chapters as we dive into some of the unconscious ways in which we sabotage or destroy healthy relationships in our lives. To move forward, we will need to make the unconscious more conscious, starting with how (and why) we make and break emotional bonds with other people.

CHAPTER 5

ATTACHMENT AND THE SELF

A Game of Cat and Mouse – *Cassie's Story* (i)*

> *'This relationship has been the most intense experience of my life. Intensely blissful, intensely painful, intensely damaging and intensely healing. It's taken me right to the edges of insanity – beyond what I thought I could bear.'*

Cassie and Aidan were on fire from the beginning. They met at a party, where they talked and flirted for an hour or so. It got late, the booze ran out and, when Aidan asked Cassie to come home with him, she felt surprised that she said . . . *yes.*

'I don't think I've ever gone home with someone just after meeting them like that, but something about his confidence, how brazen he was about what he wanted, just felt strangely irresistible. When we got into his bedroom, I couldn't stop talking and moving. Nervous, excited – you know. But he was just so . . . calm. He stretched himself out on the bed and smiled. Eventually, I found the courage to join him. We kissed and . . . we had sex. All night. It was amazing. More like a movie than real life. But when I got up the next morning to leave for work, it was like he switched gears, becoming nonchalant. I guess I assumed that was his way of making it clear he wasn't up for meeting again. I often wonder what the next few years would have been like if we had just left it there. What agony we'd have been spared. The ecstasy we'd have missed.'

Aidan messaged Cassie that afternoon, making it clear he wanted more. A week or so later, they met again and the fire reignited. Both of them marvelled at the chemistry – sex that was both explosive and respectful, and also felt quite natural. They continued to date, for several months. When they were together, they had fun, but between their meetings things weren't great. Cassie, at least, found Aidan's communication a bit unpredictable and off-kilter: one moment he was all over her, sending messages that implied he wanted to take their relationship to the next level, and the next he had gone offline for hours, or days, without explanation. When he came back, he was full on, asking to see her, because he missed her very much. If she mentioned her surprise that he was back, he would deflect, usually with sexual innuendo and compliments. If she questioned him more directly, asking why he had been silent, he became defensive – furious, even.

'Aidan had this extraordinary ability to control a conversation. Like he could just shut a topic down by ignoring the subject. The worst was when he turned my own questions or worries back on me. Like once, when I felt really insecure and asked, *Where have you been? I thought maybe there was someone else,* and he typed back, *Why are you even asking me that? Is it you? Who are you fucking?* That sort of thing happened a lot, and each time I felt myself try to challenge it and then just back down because he was so adamant, so unrelenting. Sometimes I felt my mind was bending. I thought I must be mad.'

On some level, Cassie knew that Aidan's manipulative behaviour should have sent her running. But the misery she felt when he was upset with her only made her more relieved when 'the other Aidan' came back with messages of desire and adulation. It was an intoxicating state of affairs: the bigger Cassie's craziness when he disappeared, the greater her high when he returned. Together they triggered her into an ever-anxious state. When his messages were forthcoming and complimentary, she felt great. But when they were absent or scratchy, she felt terrible, as if she had lost contact with the ground beneath her feet and would do almost anything to get it back.

They dealt with conflict differently too. When Aidan was hurt, he would lash out; he would let off steam and the fight was 'done'. For Cassie, however, his words cut deep and being on the receiving end of explosive anger left her reeling with shock for days after. Her immediate response was to recoil, and Aidan would feel rejected and go silent, retreating for hours into a physical and emotional space where he became unreachable. And Cassie, because of her own set of issues, needed to know he was coming back. In the face of silence, her distress escalated, and she would often become desperate, even hysterical, and start sending frenzied messages (into the void):

Please come back, I beg you. I'm sorry. Please. Just talk to me.

No response.

Where have you gone? I need you, now. Come back, please. I'm begging you.

No response.

How can you treat me like this? What's wrong with you?

Nothing.

This isn't fair! Fuck you, I hate you.

Nothing. Hours, maybe a day – even two – would typically pass before Aidan would re-emerge and Cassie, beyond desperate for connection, would seek reconciliation. He, however, was not so keen. Injured by Cassie's tirade, he would respond with coldness and indictments. Both felt persecuted by the other one. But how could both, then, be the victim? It was like a game of cat and mouse without clear roles. Crucially, neither of them understood *why* the other behaved the way they did, or what exactly triggered it. Because when they worked, they were beautiful. But they never worked for long.

'Those times when we were open with each other, really seeing the other person truly, were so precious to me. It was like our sex, the passion we shared and our skin-on-skin contact, literally thawed out his heart and he became more real – less suave and barbed, somehow. And when he gave me his full attention . . . it was like basking in pure sunlight after days of thick, grey cloud. He could be so beautiful – generous, funny, loving, sweet . . . But I also had this strong sense that he was really, really sad. Underneath the mask, he had these parts of himself that he hid. If I'm honest, there was something alluring for me about being the only person who saw under the mask.'

It was clear to Cassie that Aidan, for all his tendency to boast, was fundamentally unhappy with himself. Sometimes, usually in the moments after orgasm, he would show glimpses of his tender spirit – loving and childlike. But then, a glance at the clock and he could switch. Usually around a half-hour before they said goodbye, he'd go back to being dismissive: 'It was like watching someone pack their heart back into a cool box. I think a part of me knew that it was about his own insecurities, but still, it never failed to send me into a spin. I would leave feeling chaotic and self-doubting, asking myself: who was this guy, really? Which bit of him should I trust? How could someone be so dreamy and attentive one moment, but then so aloof the next? This, coupled with how fast he could fly off into a rage, meant I was always waiting for the next switch. In the end, even the good times made me worried, like it hurt to feel happy when I knew from experience it could not last. My health, my sleep, my work . . . it all started to suffer. But I couldn't help it; I needed him. He was my elixir – my heroin. Even though it was exhausting, because I was either ecstatic or despairing, I guess I assumed this was just *real love*. What else could have this crazy power? I just kept trying to make him happy. I really felt I had no choice.'

What were your reactions on reading this?

Did you negatively judge Aidan here, wonder what might be wrong with him that he would blow hot and cold so much? Maybe you thought Cassie should have just set a boundary or walked away? Perhaps you identified with one of them, having experienced what it is to be locked into this push–pull style of relationship where drama is high and trust low.

You aren't alone if you did: the dynamic above may sound extreme, but it's surprisingly common, for reasons of insecurity. Insecurity, in a relational sense, does not mean the same as insecurity in a more casual, everyday sense. It isn't about having a 'bad hair day' or just feeling a bit unsure of yourself after performing badly in a job interview. This refers to a much more entrenched type, one which involves an internalised sense of not being safe or worthy. It can often be hidden or unconscious or even normalised to such a degree that the person suffering doesn't even realise the security they lack. Then one day someone comes along who shines a mirror on them, forcing them to look and see the full extent of their precarious, insecure blueprint.

For Cassie that person was Aidan. At first, she didn't feel it, but once she began to attach to him, all her insecurities rose to the surface. Then she found herself unconsciously employing coping methods that she had learnt as a child for keeping that someone special close. Cassie started to 'enmesh' with Aidan, using him to help her feel safe inside, just as a child might their mother. When he disappeared, therefore, she felt adrift, like a small, lonely boat in the middle of a vast sea. Aidan, however, needed to disappear, either physically or emotionally, when he felt vulnerable; establishing an explicit distance meant taking back control, and made him feel safe. That made their dynamic excruciating because what made Cassie feel unsafe made Aidan feel safe, and vice-versa. Until either or both of them could instigate a massive shift, reorienting their search for safety inwards instead of outwards, their relationship was destined to be unsteady and tormenting.

Security and Insecurity – Your Attachment Style

I will never forget the day I first encountered attachment theory. It was at the beginning of my six-year journey towards qualifying as a psychotherapist and I was in a lecture hall with 100 other people, all of whom were sitting in diligent silence completing a questionnaire about how they tended to relate to others. The document outlined all sorts of possible scenarios in relationships and required us to tick whichever answer sounded most like the reaction we might have to things like conflict, miscommunication, absence, intimacy, etc. I rattled through the thing in minutes, finding it surprisingly easy to recognise myself in one of the multiple-choice answers to every question. As I totted up my scores, I became aware of a sense of panic. Something was being unearthed inside me – a powerful realisation that I felt suddenly unable to contain. My breathing became shallow, and instinctively my legs started moving as I dashed out of the lecture hall, thinking, *Help! I need fresh air*. Next thing I knew I was slumped on the pavement of a busy London Street, half wheezing and half crying.

Pieces of my past were coming together faster than I could process. Shards of memories cut my skin. What had just happened in that lecture hall? Something about that questionnaire and the preceding lecture on attachment theory made sense of so much that I had struggled with for so long. Those chronic feelings of unsafety. How I became crazed by romantic relationships, which, after a strong beginning, always descended into chaos. That familiar fear of losing myself. Equal only to the fear of being forgotten. The insecurity deep within, which was now rising to the surface.

Attachment theory – a brief introduction

Attachment theory is a model of human behaviour founded in the 1950s by British psychologist John Bowlby who pioneered the idea that the original relationship between self and other is what lays down a blueprint for future relationships in his 1969 book *Attachment and Loss, Vol.1: Attachment* – refuting the Freudian idea that human beings are essentially driven by selfish pleasure.

Bowlby believed that the drive to connect or 'attach' to other beings was universal; that it is in our nature to wish to form 'a deep and enduring bond that connects one person to another across time and space'. He insisted that we could be more or less secure in our attachments – in the way we make or break these emotional bonds – depending on our early life experiences of attachment; that is, how our caregivers* related to us. If these early attachment experiences were largely positive, with the child getting enough space and affection to develop, then an innate security builds. If these experiences were not balanced or consistent enough, however, with the child being frequently overwhelmed or dismissed, then the opposite would take place: innate insecurity forms.

On top of this, there are different types of insecurity, as intensely researched in the 1970s and 1980s by two of Bowlby's associates, Mary Ainsworth and Mary Main. By examining the behaviour of infants when separated from, and reunited with, their caregivers, these two women discovered that the ways in which we express insecure attachment can be wildly different and fall into separate categories. These categories remain the basis for much of the thinking around insecure attachment, with many scientists, particularly neuroscientists, and theorists adding to the enormous body of work done around the subject; how attachment impacts on not just our mind, but also our brain and body – the way we are wired to react.

The secure attachment

This section outlines some characteristics of what John Bowlby called 'secure attachment' or 'being securely attached'.

* 'Caregivers' feels like a rather clinical term for those who birth, feed, clothe, house and nurture babies and children, but it is also the most inclusive and descriptive term I can find for anyone who is in a parental or custodian role. Going forward, I'll use it to refer to anybody from step-parents, grandparents, guardians, elder siblings and anybody emotionally and physically close enough to a baby or child to have an influence on their attachment blueprint.

At its most basic, I think about security as having enough trust, both in oneself and in the other(s), to be able to enjoy love and connection without it being tormenting.

Security is also about self-worth. When we are secure enough inside, we can strive for high-quality relationships, rather than just accepting or rejecting whatever comes. People who grew up with a secure blueprint are neither terrified of being alone, nor devoted to it. They wander through life believing that conflict can end in repair and that one's own needs matter just as much as another adult's. Signs of secure attachment include an ability to share feelings with trusted others and to maintain relationships without huge swings in emotional proximity.

They also tend to find relationships a whole lot easier and more straightforward than other, more insecure types. They will also likely be less interested in attachment theory than insecure types, because they haven't experienced the pain and havoc that insecurity creates. These lucky ones can tolerate disappointment without collapsing. For them, feeling hurt and rejected does not necessitate a shut-down or melt-down. Of course, they are still humans; for securely attached people, life is still full of challenges and setbacks, but their solid start in life facilitates a healthier way to handle them. Those who are securely attached tend to have a better sense of self-esteem and a generally more positive world view. Thus, they ask for help and accept it; they thrive with consistent support around them and engage in self-caring behaviours and compassionate self-talk. Security is also about being able to trust ourselves and meet our own emotional needs much of the time. Trusting someone else, after all, is not about *en*trusting your entire wellbeing into their care, nor about having to be in charge of theirs.

To be fundamentally secure in relationships means that we are, for the most part, able to trust that someone who loves us still holds us in their mind and heart even when they are not physically with us or a bit preoccupied by their own shit. Security means being able to tolerate a certain level of disappointment in relationships (reality, we might call it); those times when a loved one gets it wrong. That's one reason why putting someone on a pedestal is always a terrible move. Not only does a pedestal cast a far greater shadow, but whoever is up there has a long way to fall when they inevitably make a mistake. Having a sense of innate security is about being neither above nor below those you love. It is trusting that if/when another person does hurt or disappoint you, they will return to work things out. Or that, perhaps crucially, you can tolerate it if they don't. This doesn't mean you won't feel hurt or even experience a temporary period of self-doubt as you go through challenges in your relationships. Just that your self-image remains intact.

Thankfully, most therapists believe that a more secure attachment style can be developed later in life even if we begin life insecurely. This is usually because one or more significant relationships with a friend, lover, spouse or therapist has helped them.* The word that is most commonly used is 'earnt', though I prefer to call it 'nurtured security', removing any connotations of profit or hard graft and instead highlighting the compassion and love that it takes to get to this improved position.

The insecure attachment

When it comes to love and relationships, there are all sorts of different ways that any insecure attachment can show up. These include but are not limited to: going repeatedly for the wrong kind of person; falling too fast and then changing your mind; becoming insanely jealous and

* Professor of psychiatry and attachment expert Dan Siegel says: 'The key to creating "earned security" is to make sense of our childhood; to acknowledge what was positive and what was negative; to understand how our childhood has affected our mind; and then to modify the internal models so they are more adaptive.' Quoted in Sieff, D., *Understanding and Healing Emotional Trauma: Conversations with Pioneering Clinicians and Researchers,* (Routledge, 2014), p.148.

obsessive; becoming co-dependent;* losing your autonomy; staying in abusive relationships or swerving intimacy completely. Lack of confidence, self-doubt, a predisposition to feeling unsafe and a tendency to focus on negative rather than positive potential . . . All of these traits are potential markers of insecurity, and they block our ability to make healthy and fulfilling choices.

Attachment patterns are formed during infancy and childhood, the time when we are at our most easily influenced, when we are learning how to *be*. During this phase of life, we are super vulnerable – we look to our caregivers to show and give us everything. If they are invasive, absent, abusive or just plain inconsistent and/or distracted, we can experience 'relational trauma'. Before you start thinking *But I haven't been through any real trauma,* hear me out. Trauma can be a devastating event such as the loss of a loved one or an acrimonious parental break-up, but it can also be a chronic experience that creates dysfunction or dysregulation. This might include ongoing misattunement from an inconsistent or absent parent who was unable to respond sensitively enough to their child's needs.

Trauma researcher Peter Levine offers a flexible definition of trauma as anything that overwhelms the nervous system and our ability to cope, such that it affects how we process memories. If something has had such a deep impact on you that you can re-live it in the now (and it feels real), then it's been traumatising. 'Unresolved trauma,' he writes, 'can keep us excessively cautious or inhibited, or lead us around in ever-tightening circles of dangerous re-enactment, victimisation and unwise exposure

* There are many brilliant books that have been written on co-dependency (see Suggested Further Reading, page 223) and the definition and characteristics can be complex. The condition was first addressed by Melody Beattie in her 1986 book *Codependent No More*. At its most basic, it refers to a dysfunctional need to control, enable or facilitate another in order to serve one's own deep sense of fear or insecurity.

to danger.'[*] Or, as psychiatrist and author Bessel van der Kolk puts it: 'Trauma is not the story of something that happened back then. It's the current imprint of that pain, horror and fear living inside people.'[†]

Here are just a few examples of things that would likely cause relational trauma in an infant – the kind that can later impact on their ability to bond with others in a healthy, sustainable way.

- A caregiver who is unwell or impaired in some way (e.g. subsumed by grief or post-natal depression, psychosis, OCD, PTSD or Complex PTSD).
- A caregiver with strong narcissistic traits, chronic emotional instability or who is trapped in the whirlwind of their own unresolved trauma.
- Growing up with very little touch and/or with parents who fight constantly (like Dmitri in Chapter Three, see page 64).
- Being bullied or controlled at school, at home or in the wider community.
- Repeatedly receiving little or no help with emotional regulation, such as when a baby is left to 'cry it out' or a toddler is dumped on 'the naughty step' for minutes on end to scream. Despite what some authors and doctors say about babies learning to 'self-soothe' by being ignored, it is impossible and vicious to expect this of a being whose brain is still developing. Neither a baby nor a toddler has the emotional or mental resources, nor the neurological capacity, to calm themselves down.

These are *all* potentially traumatic experiences that overwhelm our ability to cope and leave our bodies with the residue. To make matters more complex still, what might screw one person up badly could

* *Levine, P., Waking the Tiger: Healing Trauma (North Atlantic Books, 1997), p.32.*
† Van der Kolk, B., *The Body Keeps the Score: Brain, Mind and Body in the Healing of Trauma* (Penguin Random House, 2015)

leave another relatively unscathed. I believe we all come into this world with an intrinsic nature, and some are more sensitive, requiring more careful handling, than others. Despite all the variables, however, some aspects of attachment remain constant across the board. Firstly: attachment patterns are developed very early in life. Thus, security or insecurity tends to be something we start learning during childhood – an adaptive measure designed to help us survive in our environment. Secondly: this insecurity is then enhanced or healed by future relationships as we recreate aspects of what therapists call the 'primary wounding' – that important need that went unmet during our childhoods – in our adult relationships. Thirdly, until we make our attachment blueprint conscious by getting to know our automatic reactions to separation and conflict within relationships, we will likely stay stuck in, or repeat, the same dynamics. New relationships will look like old ones, as sooner or later those same old tapes start playing.

What do you remember of how you were parented? Were you left to self-soothe or were you held and acknowledged when you felt upset? Can you make links between how you were treated as a child and how you now talk to yourself? If you grew up with a caregiver who responded very negatively to you getting upset about something, or wanting affection, then you might learn to dumb down those needs in order to avoid rejection. On the other hand, if your caregiver responded apathetically to your cries unless you became loud or extremely upset, then you might learn that nobody listens – at least until you go ballistic. Maybe your caregivers could only respond to you as you needed when they themselves weren't depressed. Whatever the reason, and however understandable to an adult mind, the baby's or toddler's brain cannot rationalise away their unmet needs. All they know is that they cannot rely on getting what they need, not frequently enough anyway, and this makes them feel intrinsically insecure, like the world is not a safe (enough) place. So, they adapt, as humans do. Bending our young selves into a shape that is most acceptable, and lovable, is a brilliant survival strategy. One extreme example might be the child who, if they expressed strong feelings at home, got beaten. That child did well to repress their emotions, at least until they left home. A more subtle example might be the toddler who never has a tantrum, having learnt the one time they did that they will be shut in their bedroom until they stop crying. That toddler isn't always happy or calm, as people often assume. Rather, they have simply learnt that closeness is re-established sooner if they suppress or shut off those difficult feelings.

For many people, there comes a point where whatever shape you've bent yourself into just doesn't work anymore. Now, your beliefs and behaviours are causing you chronic pain and, most likely, making relationships tricky. The process of inquiring into your early attachment blueprint is important because it helps you understand your current struggles and open the door to change. As psychotherapist and author Esther Perel has often said in interviews and online: 'Tell me how you were loved and I will tell you how you make love.' By *make love,* I think she means how you *do* love: how you approach not only sex, but closeness and intimacy; how you go about dating, romance, togetherness and aloneness, connection and separation. In other words, it is a blueprint of how we *do* relationships, and if that blueprint is one of insecurity, then it will negatively impact on how we behave in our adult relationships, as well as who we choose as partners. The only remedy is consciousness. The more we can recognise and understand our patterns, of thought and/or behaviour, the more we can identify a choice and, from there, begin to change.

A Game of Cat and Mouse – *Cassie's story* (ii)*

Cassie and Aidan continued to love and lose one another, stuck in a break-up-make-up cycle that they could not find their way through.

Making up was beautiful – something about the honesty that emerged from their despair brought them closer – but this made the hurt even more painful.

'Every time we repaired after an awful fight, I would think, *This time we've broken through something and now we won't fight like this again*. But it just kept happening. A few days after we had seen each other, something would go wrong in our communication, one of us would react and – bang – suddenly we were back in a state of crisis.'

The problem was that the fundamental issues remained; the way each of them *did* relationships, especially conflict, had the effect of triggering insecurity in the other. One year into their relationship, Aidan and Cassie had their biggest bust-up yet. It came, as it usually did, after a small misunderstanding that escalated into a *crisis*. Aidan severed the connection for a few days and, during this time, also had sex with someone else. When the couple reconciled a fortnight later, he wanted to start again with total honesty and so told Cassie what had happened.

'I felt really crushed. I think he was surprised at how upset I was, actually. I know we'd never explicitly agreed to be exclusive, but . . . well, I just couldn't hold it in any more – I really let him see the depth of my feelings for him. He looked a bit bewildered and explained his point of view – how he had just done it for the hell of it, to make himself feel better because he was so upset about what had happened between us. He told me how, after two divorces, his faith in relationships was lower than ever and he seemed convinced that I would leave him. He kept repeating this phrase: *Love is pain – everyone leaves.* That was why he had done this, he explained: to protect himself. When I asked if he thought about my feelings at the time, he said he hadn't. I guess he didn't have much space for anyone else in all that fear. But still, it worried me. After all, how can any relationship work if one half of it is convinced it will end in tragedy?'

There was another problem here, too, which was that the more they talked, the more Aidan realised that Cassie wanted to know him for who he was, and not the grand performance he had so honed. Sounds lovely, right? Not for Aidan. He didn't want people to see him for who he truly was. He preferred the confident, public-facing version of himself to any of those softer, needier parts he had revealed during his more naked moments with Cassie. Given that he found those parts of himself so distasteful, he couldn't fathom what she saw in them.

As Cassie discovered, it is almost impossible to sustain a healthy relationship with someone who hates themselves. Self-loathing made Aidan act in destructive ways and this, of course, curtailed his ability to make fulfilling, conscious choices on both a micro and macro level. Consciously, he wanted to keep seeing Cassie, whom he adored. Unconsciously, however, he was determined to make it end, and continued to sabotage any progress by being hyper-critical and suspicious. And things went wrong, of course. Because that's what so often happens when you believe, deep down, that they will. At worst, we behave so fearfully that we actually create the very thing we fear most. At best, we are dissatisfied and unhappy. No doubt about it: Aidan was capable of deep love and connection. The problem was that it was fleeting. Or, rather, it was frequently overshadowed by his darker sides; Aidan's low self-worth and extreme need for external validation meant that nothing Cassie did would ever make him happy for long. Compliments? Affection? Loving acts or gestures? They all just fell into a bottomless hole.

If secure attachment is the gift of having a deep sense of knowing oneself to be fundamentally worth loving, then insecure attachment is the reverse: we end up dressing ourselves up with personae; manipulating, denying, people-pleasing or just hiding who we really are. Cassie did this, too, in her own way. Her desperation for reconnection with Aidan, even when he behaved destructively, demonstrates just how little she valued herself underneath. She was so busy running away from the agony of separation that she was unable to make any kind of conscious choice, like the choice to set a boundary and not allow herself to be treated like an emotional punchbag via Aidan's acting-out and projections. She looked at their relationship through what I call 'insecurity goggles': anti-corrective eyewear that blurred her view of the situation. Thanks to this skewed perspective, Cassie continued to rely on Aidan for her sense of security. Not only was he clearly *not* a good bet due to his own insecurities, but also Cassie's repeated attempts to 'save' or 'rescue' him from his sadness merely prevented both of them from helping themselves. Only Aidan could save Aidan. Only Cassie could save Cassie.

For a long and excruciating amount of time, Cassie continued to seek stability where there was none: within her relationship with Aidan. As someone who had experienced lots of early abandonment trauma, Cassie found the pain of separation from a loved one virtually intolerable, because it reopened that wound which, even in her early forties, remained unhealed.

At some point, the scales tipped: the primal agony of remaining in such a damaging dynamic became even greater than the pain of facing a lasting separation. Now Cassie's desire to unravel these alluring yet destructive relationship patterns was strong enough to bring her into therapy. Every week, for what therapists call 'the fifty-minute hour', Cassie explored her feelings and compulsions in a safe and non-judgemental space with an empathetic human being who seemed genuinely invested in what she said. Over time, she was able to notice some common themes in her life and relationships; insecure behaviours or thoughts that caused her anguish. There was the worry that her therapist would be angry with her and throw her out of therapy if she was ever unpleasant. Also, her anxiety around his going on holiday for a month: how would she survive without his support? She wanted, too, to be quite special. To be a client who stood out.

These patterns didn't operate at the same level of intensity as they did in her relationship, but clearly Cassie's relationship 'stuff' was emerging in the therapeutic dynamic. Thankfully she was able to face her fear of rejection and go further into exploring these patterns. In this safe space, they could be aired and examined, enabling her to have a new experience, since her therapist met her worries with compassion and understanding, remaining solid and interested. Here's a typical example of how therapy can help our relationships: we get to re-enact all the adaptive stuff we do 'out there' (in the world) with someone (in the therapy room) who is trained to be invested only in helping us to grow. This allowed Cassie to have a reparative experience, overlaying some of those wobbly childhood foundations with a more solid recent experience where her anxieties were met and not dismissed. Over time, Cassie was able to be honest with herself about what she truly needed and find the courage to let go. Of Aidan. Of that dynamic. And start to truly heal that wound.

It was a long and difficult process: 'Moving out of that relationship was also one of the hardest things I've ever done – so hard that it actually felt physically demanding. Getting out of bed, sleeping, eating, smiling . . . It was all just so hard without Aidan in my life. I knew we had to separate, not because I did not want him or love him, but because together we were a car crash. Still, the pull between us was so intense that leaving the relationship felt equally risky, like trying to steer my own high-speed car around a tight bend – eyes half-closed, body tensed. For months, I had to resist smashing back into Aidan. Then, finally, I felt myself relax and, although I could still feel the scars from every crash, I also knew that I'd now made it onto a straighter, more peaceful road.'

Would Cassie erase it all if she could: her love affair with Aidan? The joy and the pain? The trauma and the growth?

'I've always wanted to live a big and bold life, and that means opening up to all types of experience. To have not gone down that path with Aidan? There were a few moments when I could have skirted it, I think. But I can't imagine that the person I was back then would have chosen to take any other path. I needed to go through all that to understand what I do now. I guess that in the end I chose, quite deliberately, to let go of him – and us – for the only reason more powerful than all the reasons I had stayed so long: to save my sanity. It was the right, and only, thing to do. But also heartbreaking – beyond.'

The phrase *Can't live with them, can't live without them* springs to mind. The hard truth is this: not everyone is secure enough in themselves to be with an insecure partner. However much you love and fancy someone, they may *still* not be right for you. Perhaps the most passionate affairs are always laced with a little lunacy; it is this edge that also allows for the possibility of transformation. Clearly Aidan and Cassie facilitated a very powerful transformation in each other, one that could *not* have taken place in exactly this way with anyone else. Theirs was the most excruciating kind of love – one that was both priceless and costly, and for which they shall remain indebted to each other for years to come.

Three Typical Insecure Attachments

Bowlby and his colleagues initially regarded secure and insecure as the only two different ways of being attached. You were either one or the other, and that was probably your lot. Thankfully things have become more nuanced and hopeful since then, starting with Mary Ainsworth's 'Strange Situation'* experiment in the 1970s, which allowed for categorisation within insecure attachments.

This major piece of research examined the behaviour of twelve- to eighteen-month-old babies when temporarily separated from their mother.† First, baby and mother were placed in a new environment together – a room with toys where they could be observed by experts behind a window. Then, a stranger entered the room and started interacting with the baby. Next, the mother left the room – and her baby. After a

* I highly recommend Bethany Saltman's *Strange Situation: A Mother's Journey into the Science of Attachment* (Scribe, 2020) if you are keen to learn more about attachment and Mary Ainsworth's work.

† Please note that while Ainsworth's research was conducted with birth mothers only, attachment theorists and therapists alike now recognise that babies can develop very strong bonds with any kind of parental figure or 'caregiver'.

few minutes, the stranger also left and was replaced by the mother, who re-entered. Finally, the mother exited the room, leaving the baby completely alone.

The most important part of this experiment was to see how babies behaved when their mother returned. Some were pleased to see her, and clearly felt reassured by her presence, which provided them with 'a secure base' from which they could explore, physically and emotionally. Also, once reassured, they were able to enjoy playing again – pursuing their own interests without fear or anxiety of being left again. These children were deemed 'securely attached' or 'secure'.

There were other babies, though, who did not care much whether their mother was present or not and took a long while to 'warm up' upon her return. Ainsworth placed these children into a category she called insecure-avoidant, or 'avoidant' for short. Avoidant attachment is also sometimes called 'dismissive' since it involves deactivating the need for attachment with those special people in one's life. In adults, this style of attachment is often associated with putting on the brakes in relationships.

There was another group of babies who Ainsworth classified as 'insecure-anxious' – or 'anxious'. These babies showed relatively high levels of distress when their mother left and then were hard to reassure or settle when they returned, clearly angry or disturbed by the experience of separation. Ainsworth also used the word 'resistant' or 'anxious-ambivalent' in reference to the resistance or ambivalence these babies had to feeling soothed or reassured. Unlike the avoidant babies, anxious babies' attachment systems were hyperactivated. In adults, this style of attachment is often associated with hitting the accelerator in relationships.

There was another category of babies observed in this piece of research who fitted neither of these insecure categories, nor the secure one either. These babies' behaviour seemed more chaotic. They behaved haphazardly around their mothers, seeming all at once desperate for attention, but also fearful of it. In 1986, Ainsworth's colleague Mary Main categorised these babies as 'insecure-disorganised'.* This style involves both deactivating *and* hyperactivating the need to be close or stay connected. In adults, it is therefore often associated with hitting the brake and accelerator simultaneously in relationships.

Avoidant attachment

Avoidant attachment – sometimes called insecure-avoidant or dismissive.

Avoidant attachment is often portrayed as the bad guy of the insecure attachment styles, the one associated with self-aggrandisement, mercilessness and even extreme actions like "ghosting", where a person suddenly drops off radar with no warning or explanation. But really that's not fair: to say an avoidant person is malicious is a bit like saying that clouds are being nasty when they rain. Much better to think of it as a reaction to certain conditions: the avoidant turns their connection dial down when they are stressed or feel unsteady, whereas the anxiously attached person turns their dial up. In their dialled-down state, the avoidant person, particularly if unconscious about what's going on attachment-wise, is simply unable to connect, especially with an anxious partner who needs a high level of engagement, which is overwhelming for the avoidant. Underneath all that surface-level composure, however, the avoidant person is in pain. It's the kind of blank pain that can be recognised via feeling nothing, the sense of being behind some glass. It isn't that they don't care, but that at this point in time they are fundamentally disconnected from themselves. Give them space and compassion and they'll return when they are ready.

*Please note: all insecure styles of relating come under the umbrella of 'insecure attachment', so people can oscillate between the different insecure styles, particularly from avoidant to anxious and vice-versa, depending on each individual relationship and the context around it.

Anxious attachment

Anxious attachment – sometimes called 'resistant' (in infants) or 'pre-occupied' (in adults).

Those with anxious attachment styles usually had unreliable parents – loving and supportive, but available one minute and unavailable the next. They never internalised enough security to go out in the world feeling solid and, as a result, struggle to trust. Unlike those displaying an avoidant style of attachment, people exhibiting an anxious hyperactivated style tend to play up their need for connection, pulling others towards them when they are threatened, stressed or dysregulated (struggling to control or settle their emotional state). By "play up", I don't mean dramatise – although anxious people can certainly take dramatic action to get their needs met – but more that this need is heightened and the volume's up.

Why would somebody develop anxiety and hyperactivation as a regulating strategy? Isn't it more dysregulating? Yes, but if ramping up distress was the only way of being seen and heard by their preoccupied or inconsistent caregiver then it's also a solution. It's a technique learnt young, back when getting needs met felt essential. For a baby who can't yet feed or clothe themselves, knowing the whereabouts of your caregiver can be literally life or death. A baby doesn't know if their caregiver has just popped next door for five minutes or gone away forever. No wonder their distress can quickly reach epic proportions.

For the anxiously attached adult, sensations and emotions associated with abandonment can feel just as terrifying now as they did then, even when the mind *knows* there is no danger. Often they manifest as panic attacks or paranoia; the physical awareness that *something's wrong.* That's why this attachment style shows up as the frequent need for contact, from touch to texts; physical and verbal reassurances that everything is okay and, *Yes, I am still here.* Those with this kind of attachment style can quickly go from being articulate, autonomous adults, like Cassie, to fragmented and childlike. An anxious person's internal voice usually bolsters their attachment, which suggests the object of their affection is losing interest or can't be trusted; *They think I'm needy and pathetic and clearly don't want me anymore.*

It is the task of the anxious person, then, to be able to (re)parent that young child within who becomes so very distressed in adult relationships. If this sounds a bit esoteric, then just remember that we literally hold unresolved trauma on a cellular level. This kind of reparenting work is sometimes referred to as 'inner-child work' and is beneficial also to those with any signs of avoidance. Even securely attached people are not immune from childhood wounds and may find inner-child work healing.*

Ultimately, the anxiously attached person's challenge is to become more self-reliant, developing a clear sense of their own feelings and thoughts, and learning to trust themselves and their ability to keep themselves safe when they are distressed or dysregulated. They would do well to pick a secure partner, if possible, who is capable of reassuring them when they are anxious without negating their own needs.

Fearful-avoidant attachment

Fearful-avoidant attachment – where high levels of both anxiety and avoidance co-exist.

While those with avoidant or anxious attachment patterns showed a consistent way of behaving insecurely in relationships in Ainsworth's

* This work can be very deep and should be undertaken with the support of a trained therapist or, if in a group setting, with a trained facilitator. There are also some excellent books and workbooks on the subject, which can kickstart or support exploration. See the appendix for recommendations.

studies, those with the so-called disorganised pattern were far less predictable. To put it another way, for these babies – whose caregivers were so completely inconsistent – there was no best way to adapt in order to get their needs met. In 1991, researchers Kim Bartholomew and Leonard Horowitz built on this idea of disorganised attachment and suggested an adult version of this style that was not necessarily as chaotic and unpredictable as disorganised attachment, but was based on having a more consistent style that included strong tendency towards both avoidant *and* anxious traits. They called it 'fearful avoidant', suggesting this was when someone simultaneously (or in very quick succession) displayed high levels of anxiety and high levels of avoidance. This can look very similar to operating from a totally disorganised blueprint, and certainly, the two terms are used synonymously in a lot of online articles. The fearful-avoidant style is a little more consistent, however, since there *is* an organising principle. That principle is fear, where the terror of not being loved by others is equalled only by the terror of it happening. More simply for these types, when activated or triggered, love = terror. Those who experience this kind of fearful-avoidant attachment describe it as like being at war with one's own needs, simultaneously trying to grow roots whilst also desperate to take off.

It is the task of anyone with this kind of blueprint to be especially gentle with themselves and, if possible, with those who love them. Avoiding relationships is not the answer, even though they are a source of pain, but neither is losing yourself in them. Developing consistent and trusting relationships at a pace that feels manageable is essential here, as is learning to communicate (and recognise) your own needs. These types would, unsurprisingly, do well to find a secure partner who is clear on their own boundaries in the face of pressure, has benefited from a solid support network and will pay that forward for the disorganised person.

Attachment and the Self – In Essence

Attachment issues are complex and deep-rooted. Their foundations lie in childhood, and in adulthood, they often present as something less obvious, like generalised anxiety, depression, loneliness, obsessions and compulsions and/or addictions.

Your attachment style is a bit like your own personal schema for how you "do" or "don't do" relationships. It includes how you react to separation, or conflict, and how you go about getting your needs met and defending yourself from hurt. From a place of secure attachment, you can give and receive more nourishment in almost all aspects of life. The more an insecurely attached person nurtures inner security (via different therapies, movement practices, bodywork and any kind of cognitive self-development work), the more freely they are able to make choices from a regulated, conscious place, rather than simply reacting. Reaction = blueprint 'style'. Response = choice.

Attachment and the Self – Inquiry

Think about what the word *attachment* conjures up for you. Pay attention to any knee-jerk thoughts and feelings you experience. What phrases or images come to mind when you think of being *attached* to or *bonded* with another person?

Other questions that might help include:

- Do you feel generally good about the whole being-close-to-others thing?
- Do you tend to believe that people will be responsive to you, there for you and can be relied upon (within reason) most of the time?
- Do you assume that people don't care and just not bother sharing yourself?
- Do you worry that they will leave, or that you are too much, not enough or wrong?

Have you figured out which attachment style is most familiar to you? Maybe you can see different styles at different points and with various people in your life. If you'd like to deepen your inquiry, consider the following questions and go off your gut response. The first six are characteristic of the anxious attachment style, the second six of the avoidant, and the third six pertain more to the fearful. Please note, however, that typecasting always risks generalisation. Everyone is different and people change as life goes on.

When I feel unsure of myself, or you, or us, I . . .

- cause an argument so that I can storm out, cry, break/make up with you.
- seethe quietly and drop really subtle hints about my need for reassurance.
- call you and message you incessantly about things to reassure myself you still love and desire me.
- start going through your social media accounts and emails for clues that you are leaving or more generally seek evidence that you are going off me.
- agree to things I don't really want to do because I feel the need to please you and am afraid of losing you.
- become extremely angry or frustrated if you don't immediately "get" what I am feeling or respond to it in a sensitive way.

When I feel unsure of myself, or you, or us, I . . .

- stop replying so quickly, or at all, to your messages and calls.
- make myself really busy so we can't spend so much quality time together.
- mentally put you, and us, into a separate box from the rest of my life.
- tell myself to stop being stupid/there's no point in raising my concerns as you will not react well, or listen, or be interested in me at all.

- start thinking obsessively about an ex, remembering only the good bits so that they compare favourably to you.
- follow the compulsion to sabotage our relationship or distance myself by engaging with another person in a way that our relationship does not allow for.

When I feel unsure of myself, or you, or us, I . . .

- behave in ways that do not follow a specific pattern: sometimes being very clingy and at others just shutting off. This can happen in very quick succession.
- go totally flat and "lose" a couple of hours, after which I realise I have been staring at a wall.
- have a strong urge to be close to, and far from, you. I just don't know what the hell I want. I don't even know for sure which bits are real.
- find it impossible to express myself. It's like the words are trapped inside, or else there is absolutely no language at all.
- have a strong desire to hurt myself in some way, or to numb out completely to take the edge off.
- feel simultaneously furious with you and also devastated that you aren't here.

Now What?

This chapter is a biggie. I've introduced the idea of attachment and outlined the main ways that insecurity presents itself in relationships. Perhaps you have recognised an insecure style of relating in yourself or someone you love. Always remember that insecure attachment is a protective mechanism developed when young in order to maintain safety (and survive). You cannot blame yourself for anything you did when unconscious of these mechanisms. You can, however, take responsibility, and that means committing to a deeper, long-term inquiry into how you behave when triggered into insecurity. The question, *Yes, okay, but what do I do about this?* is a common one. Right now, you just keep reading and stay hopeful. Remember, patterns *can* shift, but real change takes real time. Let's change the focus slightly from interior to exterior, looking more specifically at how insecure blueprints relate to each other, and how you can work towards security.

CHAPTER 6

ATTACHMENT AND CHOICE

When Styles Collide

What happens when we put specific styles together, particularly in a romantic relationship? Sometimes it works okay. Secure + secure, for example, is a flat road – there are unlikely to be any major attachment-related issues that mess with love and harmony. Secure + insecure can work well, too, a bit like an undulating train ride in the country that rises and falls in rhythm. Insecure + insecure, however, can be very destructive indeed, like riding a rollercoaster 24/7, with plenty of noise, sickness and panic.

Things get really difficult when two people have completely differing strategies for managing their attachment issues, particularly in 'the anxious-avoidant dance' where one member of a couple is avoidant and the other anxious. Like any dance, it relies on both people taking the right steps – here's an example of how it works:*

* These steps are just representative of typical moves forward and back in the anxious-avoidant attachment dance and are by no means conclusive. The book *Attached: Are You Anxious, Avoidant or Secure? How the science of adult attachment can help you find – and keep – love* by Amir Levine and Rachel Heller has plenty more on this particular combination, specifically as it relates to dating, love and romance.

- Avoidant person feels their sense of self threatened. Their need for connection is deactivated in order to restore internal safety.
- Before there is time to establish the cause of the avoidant's withdrawal or allow them time to come forward again, anxious person freaks out and their nervous system goes into fight-or-flight mode. *(Internal sirens wail. Threat! Abandonment in sight!)*
- Anxious person desperately tries to reconnect. This is either in an overt way, expressing or demanding a need for contact and reassurance, or in a covert, potentially seductive way, trying to instigate jealousy or an argument, for example. It is all an attempt at restoring internal safety by means of gaining reassurance from the other.
- Avoidant person feels even more overwhelmed and further withdraws.
- Anxious person freaks out more, feels desolate and ignored, so adopts regulating strategy (of hyperactivating attachment system) even more and hypes up their demands by threatening, desperate or pleading communication.
- Avoidant person is completely overwhelmed and unable to respond in the way the anxious person needs. Instead, they adopt their regulating strategy of avoiding a response completely. Turns phone off, goes home, falls asleep, etc.
- Anxious person loses it. Does something to incite a reaction in the avoidant.
- Avoidant person may feel hurt, so cuts off anxious person.
- Anxious person begs for forgiveness and plays down all their needs so as to win the avoidant back.
- Avoidant returns, and all is okay, though both are wary and insecure. Just a matter of time before it happens again.

This cycle, or any similar version of it, can go on for months, even years. Sometimes the anxious or avoidant behaviours that each person exhibits in these dynamics actually become a major part of their personality and the 'dance' outlined above becomes a defining feature of a relationship's shape and identity.

It *is* possible that an anxious and avoidant couple could have a positive relationship where they develop a secure attachment to one another and increase security within. If you look again at the above list of steps, you can probably find opportunities when a change in one person's behaviour could stop the whole damned dance midway. Those early relationship dynamics are often sought in later connections in the hope that *this time will be different.* Many therapists believe that this is no accident: we unconsciously pull towards us those people or relationships that will force us to look at what needs to change inside us.*

This takes work; one or both people will need to recognise their defence/coping mechanisms in the face of loss. They would need to be willing to see things from a very different point of view and be committed to moving out of their comfort zone in order to accommodate the need for space or connection in their partner.

More often than not, however, the anxious-avoidant combination is carnage. It's not just the collision of two opposing reactions to similar wounds, but the very existence of such wounds themselves that causes the issues. That's why awareness is so important. First, the wounds must be identified. Then they'll probably start to bleed, and we must make a choice to move towards healing, and away from further damage. As psychotherapist Alan Downs writes in his book *The Velvet Rage*, 'Two deeply wounded people cannot form a healthy relationship. They may struggle, compromise and even stay together, but until each heal their

* Why would anyone, even unconsciously, recreate a painful experience or dynamic from their childhood? For all the same reasons that we return to an instrument we haven't mastered or a riddle we haven't solved: so that we can finally succeed at it, or at least fail better. Freud called this 'the repetition compulsion' – the idea being that if we can drag that wounding experience from the depths of our past right back up to the surface with a current relationship then maybe we can do it differently. Then, and only then, can we start swimming with choice on the horizon.

own wounds the relationship will always be a struggle.' The problem for Cassie and Aidan was not so much that they both had an insecure attachment style, but that those styles were quite different and the initial wounds that prompted their development were as yet too unhealed to cope with their re-wounding.

From Insecurity to Security

Given time and commitment, an insecure attachment blueprint can begin to look more like a secure one. The more we learn to tolerate our uncomfortable feelings of anxiety or shame, the less we will need to engage in self-defeating behaviours or relationships that keep us running from our wound.

My own struggle with insecure attachment has been huge. It has permeated many stages of my life, taking a predominantly anxious style with occasional swings towards avoidance. There was the stage when, aged four, I clung to my mother every morning at school drop-off, desperate not to be left, and then felt miserable, sometimes beside myself, all day. I remember this well: sitting in the basement at the lunch table, with the other children playing together, feeling so totally unsafe in my fragile young bones because *something is wrong – I don't feel safe without my mummy.* After a disastrous trip away from home when I was seven, I became very anxious and, even months after returning, could not stay a single night away. I wanted more than anything to stay close to home, and to my mother; to cling to her in case we were to be separated in that terrifying way again. On the other hand, I remember swinging the other way during my teens and becoming avoidant of the intimacy that I so clearly longed for. I remember how one day, when I was sixteen, I decided on a whim to dump my first boyfriend at sixteen. My reason? I really liked him and found it too painful to know it wouldn't last; that we were young and he especially was very busy at weekends with sport, meaning we didn't see much of each other.

And how, just one year later, I ended my safe and happy relationship with a caring young man because he was just too perfect. I thought I was bored. I thought it wasn't right. But, looking back, I can see that really it was more that the security felt unfamiliar. And I felt undeserving of it.

I didn't question my choices much back then, but I did have a sense that it was strange – the way I longed to be close to someone but, despite being presented with clear evidence that I was actually getting what I wanted, I became terrified and pushed them away. I also found it hard to stick to any one job or career path, constantly seeking something 'out there' that might finally fix me and make me feel better 'in here'. I wanted to feel seen. Except then, during my first opportunity as a teen to sit opposite a kindly school counsellor, who was asking questions about my feelings, I felt invaded and ran away. It took another fourteen years before I sat in any kind of therapy chair again, by which time I had tried and tested other methods to push away my difficult feelings of longing and nostalgia. These included long-distance running, starving, bingeing, cigarettes and booze. After several unsuccessful attempts, I eventually got sober at twenty-nine. I think of this as the end of my drinking, but just the beginning of my very messy and beautiful healing journey. I say 'the beginning' because, without my anaesthetising nightly bottle of wine, I really had to feel my feelings. Now I was faced with the sadness – a kind of unwashed and uncooked grief – that pulsed through my blood from the moment I woke to the instant I went to sleep.

I learnt pretty fast that if I was to remain sober, which I truly wanted to, I needed to deal with all those underlying feelings, the unbearable ones that led me to drink, eat, diet or exercise obsessively as addictive distractions from the pain.* Those painful feelings had arrived, consciously at least, after that disastrous trip away from home when I was seven.

* The idea that addiction is a distraction from pain is explored insightfully and in depth by the famous doctor, author and addictions expert Gabor Maté. He often urges that we 'don't ask, why the addiction? Ask: why the pain?'

There was that free-floating melancholy, a sense both of being faraway from other people, and of having lost something essential, which surrounded me when alone. Also, the fear that followed me everywhere: the certainty that I wasn't safe inside my skin; that at any point my emotions could knock me over and roll me around just like a big, frothy wave. But most of all there was the craving. The craving for arms and skin and warmth. For someone to take care of me, forever. Which was, almost certainly, not long enough.

I didn't feel safe just by myself. I had a certain confidence and articulateness, but deep inside I was insecure. No wonder I searched, via people, substances and behaviours, to feel safe. The problem was it never lasted. Drugs and alcohol wore off the next day, and endorphins are temporary and did little to soothe me anyway. Honing my physique, too, was a red herring. The better the outside looked, the more perfectionist I became, until the only thing that my body reflected was my never-good-enough self-image.

Clearly the problem was within and would not be sorted with a flatter stomach or a bigger bank balance. And as for finding security via other people? That was hit and miss. Hit: groups (of friends or recovering addicts). Miss: any single one other person. The truth is, there is no *one* perfect human who can cure you of insecurity. The only one who can help you is *you.* The wound is within, and so's the healing.

So how, then, do we do it?

For me, it has been an ongoing practice. Just because I work as a therapist and have come a long way on my personal journey towards security doesn't mean I'm 100 per cent *there.* In truth, I have long stopped expecting to reach the holy grail of secure attachment. I am more invested in laying down secure attachments over the top of my historic insecure one, rather than seeking to eradicate that early attachment wounding completely. What has worked for me is combining long-term psychotherapy with other self-development tools like reading, journaling, exercising, dancing, sharing, practising regular yoga and meditation *and also* going out and having relationships with people. This is very important: without the practice of relating to others, we can't make an embodied change. Patterns change by being noticed, and then altered. They cannot be altered without an opportunity arising, and an opportunity will arise from a trigger. But there are no points for punishment. You get to choose how fast you go.

The first thing we need to learn is how to recognise when our insecure attachment gets triggered. One simple test I use is to assess how urgent something feels. Generally speaking, the more urgent it feels that you get your needs met, the more reactive you are. Let's say you have an upsetting exchange with your partner on the phone and the conversation ends badly. The anxiously attached person will default to spiralling upwards, becoming hyperactivated and maybe firing off a series of calls and texts immediately after the phone goes down. They feel a desperate need to reconnect and get some answers *right now or else.* The avoidantly attached person conversely spirals downwards, becoming deactivated, putting their buzzing phone in another room, distancing themselves from the upset or conflict. Most probably they are feeling a desperate need to withdraw and disconnect *right now or else.* Both people are overwhelmed by their feelings in that moment – they just have opposite ways of dealing with them.

It's not that you shouldn't ever have those reactive feelings. Chances are you might always experience them to some degree however much work you do on your attachment patterns. Trust me when I say that I'm in contact with my own anxious attachment a lot. Its negative impact on my relationships, however, is diminishing as I'm learning to watch my instantaneous feelings and thoughts and not always react to them. After all, it's not the thoughts or sensations themselves, but the need to act and behave in a certain way *right now or else* that causes the problems. Being able to sit with a certain level of discomfort when you're feeling upset with someone, *while also not severing or demanding anything*, is a good sign of security. However, this is a process of ongoing inquiry rather than an overnight quick fix.

Here are some suggestions for when insecure attachment is triggered:

- When I'm upset or anxious I'll ask myself, *What would a secure person do? If I felt safe with any potential emotions that might arise, if I was not worried about being left, or being ignored, what would I say or do right now?*
- *What would a secure person do?* can also be applied to someone triggered into avoidant-dismissive or fearful-avoidant attachment. *If I felt able to honour my needs right now, what would I say or do? If I felt it was safe to tell the truth about how I'm feeling rather than hide, what might I ask for?* When avoidant attachment flares up, we tend to become completely overwhelmed and believe the only remedy is withdrawal. Taking small risks can help you move towards security, such as asking for the space you need and reminding the other person you're coming back.
- Consider the acronym FEAR. False Evidence Appearing Real. Whether we are triggered into anxious or avoidant attachment, craving immediate reassurance or immediate withdrawal, we are in a fear-based state. Finding a way to identify and, if appropriate, communicate that fear, rather than demand for it to be removed or pushed away, is essential for anyone struggling with insecure attachment of any type.
- For someone triggered into anxious attachment, the tape inside the mind says something like, *I can't cope, help!* For someone triggered into avoidant attachment, the tape inside the mind says something like, *I can't cope, go away!* Find a safe and sacred space where you can go and reconnect with yourself and your environment. This helps those with any kind of attachment insecurity to return to their personal safe zone before they re-enter the relationship zone.

- 'Square breathing' is a simple and quick way of soothing a hyper-activated nervous system and focusing on something benign, like counting. Inhale for four counts, hold your breath for four, exhale for four counts, then hold for four counts before starting again. Repeat ten times at least.
- If you're emotionally dysregulated, and/or in fight-or-flight mode, you are unlikely to be thinking clearly. Regulation, therefore, is the primary goal, and after that you can start making sense of what might have just happened. So, if you are feeling insecure, or notice that you are struggling to manage your emotions, start by focusing on the sensations instead of the story. By this I mean name – ideally out loud – what is happening in your body ('My heart is racing,' for example), rather than allowing your mind to create a story from that sensation ('It's been four hours since they last texted, I think I'm about to get dumped').
- Move your body and shift energy around. For very good evolutionary reasons, stress hormones build when we are in fight-or-flight 'survival' mode. The idea is that, when we sense that a sabre-toothed tiger is nearby, we get a sudden surge of adrenaline and can run faster than ever (hopefully faster than the tiger), whether the tiger is real or perceived. Exercise reduces the body's levels of stress hormones and releases endorphins (natural painkillers), which help to make you feel better. Don't overdo it, though!

For those who are predisposed towards insecurity, achieving security is a bit like becoming a yogi; it is something that we have to practise as well as learn; it involves both the body and the mind and requires a lot of dedication. We will have good days and bad days. Some relationships help us to heal, triggers and all, and others are just too triggering or destructive for our nervous systems to bear and we must choose the 'me' over the 'us'. For those who have grown up around unhealthy, enmeshed or co-dependent relationships, it can take a while to figure out where the difference lies because we didn't ever learn what 'healthy', respectful intimacy feels like.

There is no magic switch that can provide the insecurely attached individual with that enviable sense of solidity within themselves. Going against old patterns can be hard graft and take some time, a bit like pushing a boulder uphill. But you *can* push a boulder uphill, provided you take enough breaks and are supported along the way. For myself and many others I have known, working through attachment insecurities has been transformative. It impacts not just on the way one does relationships with others (pretty important), but also with yourself (vital). There is nothing more important than how you treat, relate or speak to yourself. You are the only person absolutely guaranteed to wake up with you every single morning for the rest of your choice-ist life.

Nurturing Adult Security: Developing Your Safety Web

Nobody – repeat, nobody – ever has all their attachment needs met. My favourite lecturer at therapy school insisted that the average four-year-old has an attachment need every twenty seconds! Her point was that even the most attuned parent couldn't meet all these needs – at least not without totally neglecting everything else that a four-year-old also needs their caregiver to deal with in order to make the world safe(r). Ergo: none of us will get our needs met all the time. Some of us will get our needs met some/enough of the time. And some of us will get them met some/not enough of the time.

The twentieth-century psychologist Donald Winnicott discussed the idea of 'good enough' caregiving, which meets needs with enough regularity to create security, and also helps the baby learn to tolerate their own distress as they grow up. So how much is 'enough'? It's a crucial question and the answer may vary from each individual. If you identify heavily with one of the insecure attachment styles, then the chances are your needs weren't met enough for whatever reason. You had to adapt, most probably far too early, and that did not set you up for resilience – i.e. a healthy ability to tolerate disappointment or setbacks without a loss of faith or self-image.

If we are to have successful, intimate relationships in adulthood, we have to be able to tolerate a certain level of distress. Even if we are in a very communicative relationship where both parties are pretty clued up on their 'stuff' and how to manage it, disappointment is inevitable. We will hurt others and they will hurt us, whether intentionally or not. Even the closest friend can be self-centred. Even the best sister can be too busy during a crazy time at work. The best mother can be exhausted, and even the best version of you can be reactive and take offence.

The trick to nurturing security as an adult is *not* to develop a dependency on one thing, but in fact to cultivate a collection of healthy relationships and activities that knit together strongly enough to catch you when you fall. Yes, a single relationship, such as with a therapist, might do wonders for your healing, but ultimately to sustain innate security you will need more than any one thing/person. I call this your 'Safety Web' – see an example below – referring to a changeable conglomeration of activities, people or beliefs that help you to stay grounded and connected. It's useful to make conscious what these things are, so you can remind yourself what you need. Questions to ask yourself when sketching out your own Safety Web include: what things or people bring you back to a place of greater security? What cultivates security and joy in your life? You might also like to make a list of *no-nos* for when you are feeling insecure: things that only make you wobblier, but that you can do once you feel safer.

A Safety Web

- Weekly therapy sessions. Spending time with my cat without distractions.
- Having a bath. Meditating. Sitting by my favourite old tree in the park.
- Going to the community garden and turning my phone off for half an hour.
- Telling at least one person the truth about how I'm feeling – Simon? Zoe? Grace?
- Asking for a hug from a safe person.
- Scrawling all my fears and worries out in my journal.
- Yoga class. Audio recordings of guided relaxations.
- Reading that book I found comforting (the one about self-care).
- Watching re-runs of my favourite TV show.

No-nos

- Really busy public transport and/or noisy people or places.
- Drinking alcohol or being around drunk people.
- Picking up the phone to *that* dramatic friend.
- Sharing my feelings with anyone who tends to be dismissive of emotions.
- Listening to extremely emotive music or songs that hold significance for me.
- Overexercising/exhausting myself.
- More than two cups of coffee per day.

Insecurity and Choice

Fact: a person's choices are limited if they are insecure. How can we really engage with the plethora of options available to us when we are fundamentally ruled by fear? Becoming more secure in yourself is one of the most important pieces of choice-ist work you can do, because we cannot consciously make any important change if we are doing it out of anxiety or avoidance. We can only see all the available options from a vantage point closer to security.

Nurturing security within yourself is absolutely the priority; it is also important to understand your partner'(s)' attachment style too. I believe it's never too soon to do this, and the impressions of those first few months can often give us lots of clues. I'm not suggesting you kick off with a question about attachment styles on your first date, but that you bear in mind that insecure ways of relating will have a bigger negative impact on your relationship if you aren't aware of them. If you feel uneasy, like someone is pushing you away one day and then pulling you close the next, then notice it. Lots of books on relationships will tell you to steer well clear of anyone who shows any kind of erratic behaviour when it comes to attachment. To me, that's dangerous, demeaning talk: those with insecure attachment are trying to relate to another in a way that feels safe and familiar to them. How can we learn together if we toss one another aside at the first sign of trouble? Refusing to date anyone with a remotely avoidant blueprint (because yours is clearly anxious), or steering clear of anybody with an anxious blueprint (because yours is avoidant), is like refusing to eat grapes because you've recently given up wine: you miss out on something delicious because of its potential to ferment. Better to keep an eye on the raw ingredients, checking in regularly on whether they are turning into something less healthy for you and beginning to sour in some way. Getting to know a loved one's protective strategies and making some allowances for them can be a beautiful and bonding thing. In order to do this, however, we need to keep communicating with one another and, even more important, keep communicating with ourselves.

The task here is to get to know your own trigger points so that, if another person repeatedly touches them, you can reflect on it and ideally then work together towards change, which, if not forthcoming, may of course signal that this relationship isn't nourishing. Some people aren't able or ready to do the necessary work to reorientate themselves towards security, and although it's sad, it might be best to detach, gently, from these lovers.

All through this process, the more you can focus on nurturing security within yourself, the more chance you have of working together to create a mutually fulfilling relationship. This is not to suggest that it is your job to pre-empt or second-guess any partner's needs, more that intimacy thrives off our feeling of being seen and understood. It's not easy, but it helps. Try to think of ways that other people manage their insecurity as a reflection on them and not you. Once you do this, you can step back and ask the all-important question: is this relationship working for me? It needn't be perfect all the time, but it ought to be *good enough* for you, right now.

When things get rough in a relationship, we need to know we are *choosing* to stay in it. Ask yourself if it is worth persevering. Or are you merely sleepwalking towards misery, just sort of hoping it'll work out? We cannot forcibly change another person, nor can we make them move more quickly towards security. All we can do is work on ourselves and reflect on what we will or won't accept. There are always compromises to make. Be clear about your boundaries; what is or isn't a hard limit. When we know this, we can stop viewing these boundaries as a problem and begin to see them as a choice.

Everybody's breaking point is different here. For example, something that I know I need in a romantic relationship is time together, in person. I can go without lots of phone conversations, can deal with a fair amount of moodiness and forgetfulness . . . But without a real emphasis on physicality, I become unhappy. Touch is extremely important to me. I know from bitter experience that periods of months-long physical separation are agonising, regardless of how many video calls might be shared. Whereas I have a friend who lives in the UK; her boyfriend lives in Australia, and they happily spend (only) four months of the year together. My nightmare = something she embraces.

Choice and Attachment – In Essence

Looking at relationships through the lens of attachment styles can help you get clear on what you need to do to facilitate even more choice. It also goes a long way to explaining why some dynamics are so hard to crack. There is certainly a time to step back and focus on self-healing, but ultimately we can't delve into our own attachment patterns until we push them up against someone else's. If we do not practically explore our tendencies in our relationships, and make explicit our assumptions, then we may simply continue to follow old scripts laid down in childhood, e.g. *People I love leave; Everyone needs too much from me; Nobody is interested in my feelings; I cannot trust anyone, ever; I have to be perfect to deserve love; I'm not allowed to have feelings* and many, many more. I believe there is a direct correlation between how unconsciously we recreate these old dynamics and scripts, and how unable we feel to make healthy, fulfilling choices.

Choice and Attachment – Inquiry

How can we recognise when our reaction to someone or something is the result of insecure attachment, and how might we subvert it? Ask yourself now: *How urgent is my need to react? And is that reaction familiar to me? Is it something I do specifically when I feel threatened or as if I'm losing control over someone or something?*

Now ask yourself: *Can I tolerate this uncomfortable feeling a bit longer, without reacting in that knee-jerk way?*

What helps you to calm down, or to come back, when you are anxious or wanting to disappear? Everyone has their own preferred methods and knowing them shouldn't be taken for granted. They aren't always profound; sometimes they're things as simple as breathing exercises, taking a bath or completing a repetitive administrative task. You find this in mindfulness and meditation. Blocking out noise and distraction is the path to becoming centred and more open. Once re-regulated, you have the capacity to start the more complicated work of ascertaining what you really need and how you'd prefer to express yourself.

Useful questions to ask yourself include:

- Why do I think I'm behaving in this way? What is my motivation? What am I trying to achieve with this behaviour? That is: what is beneath the words I'm saying, or the things I'm doing?
- What's the fear – the fear that is making me behave this way or say these things?
- And where might that fear come from? Is it reminiscent of something old? What age, or stage, was I at when I first felt a similar fear? When did I first become aware of it? Is this really related to what is happening now or am I superimposing the past onto the present without checking on facts first?
- Is there anything I can identify, having looked at my relationship patterns and repeated challenges, that might be trying to sort itself out? Is there something that I might (consciously or unconsciously) be trying to 'fix' or change about myself or my world view?

Let's look more specifically now at those most crucial relationships in your life and what style of attachment you suspect you have in each. You might find you display different styles of attachment in different relationships. Scribble down some things without overthinking it.

See the table below for examples:

Person	**Relationship to me**	**Attachment style**	**Behaviours and thoughts that signify it**	**More secure ways I could approach the relationship instead**
Mum	Family	Secure	Feel able to ask for and offer help, don't spend much time worrying about it. Feel okay with not hearing from her for days, know she still loves me, etc.	N/A
Annie	Adult daughter	Anxious	Very preoccupied by worries that she's not okay, which stop me doing my work. When reassured it doesn't really 'go in', and I just feel I need more reassurance.	Seek therapy to help me work on my attachment issues instead of projecting onto daughter. Explain to her that it isn't that I don't trust her, more that I don't trust myself to deal with my feelings. Reassure her it isn't her responsibility to take care of me.
Joey	Boyfriend	Avoidant	Feel need for space often, usually after we are intimate. I frequently feel so overwhelmed by the thought of communicating with him that I actually ignore his messages and zone out in front of the TV.	Explain that I do want us to be connected, but I need a little more space to come back to myself first.

Person	**Rela-tionship to me**	**Attach-ment style**	**Behaviours and thoughts that signify it**	**More secure ways I could approach the relationship instead**
Dad	Family	Fearful avoid-ant	Want Dad to get in touch with me, but when he does I don't pick up the phone or reply. Feel simulta-neously abandoned and invaded by him. Fantasise about big hug from him but then avoid it like crazy. Love to hate him, hate to love him.	Remind myself that the fearful avoidance is based on the past and not right now. This fear is in my body. Name the sensations and take the time I need. Allow myself to keep father at healthy distance with-out going silent on him.

Look again and see if you notice any patterns. I know myself that if I'm going to get stuck in my anxious attachment style, it'll invariably be in either romantic partnerships or with some kind of authority figure or boss. It rarely happens within friendships or with colleagues. For relationship anarchists (as outlined in Chapter Two, see page 49) these distinctions would be less important, since the lines between friendship and romance are deliberately refuted, and that's okay. It will be useful to notice where your hotspots are and then to move more slowly in those relationships so you can pick up each small trigger and deal with them at the time.

Now What?

The last two chapters have been very heavy on information and examples. Now, try putting some small things into action by using some of the tools above to nurture security within and notice how it has an impact, small or large, on your closest relationships. How we attach to one another affects not just our relationships, but also how we navigate our way through the world when under pressure or challenged to conform in a way that doesn't serve us. In the next two chapters, we'll be looking at some of the ways our choices can be hidden, not just by our own controlling, protective strategies, but by those of wider society too.

CHAPTER 7

CHOICE AND THE SHADOW

No Choice for the Chosen One – *Dominic's Story**

'My life was steeped in the rules of the religion that we followed. I suppose you might say that I grew up with a whole narrative around choice, which was that so much of my life simply wasn't my choice – it was God's choice.'

Dominic, thirty-one, was brought up by two extremely religious and intellectual alcoholics. The ramshackle Edinburgh townhouse in which they lived was stuffed head to toe with books; bottles clinked inside the bins. His mother, who had suffered an extraordinarily traumatic childhood involving the most hideous abuse imaginable, was a fractured and disturbed woman. She was an atheist in her youth, but a series of miscarriages followed by a very difficult birth (Dominic arrived eight weeks early – a hazardous delivery, during which both mother and baby nearly died) left her quite sure that miracles happened.

As soon as she was out of hospital, Dominic's mother went to visit the local Catholic church to give thanks to the God whom she believed had spared them both. There she found something she needed, and quickly became an integral part of the community and a daily participant at Mass. Dominic's father also became very religious, though his job as an academic kept him away from home a lot. Both parents instilled in Dominic that he should strive for perfection and piety. As an altar boy who attended Mass at least once a day, Dominic always wore a suit and polished black shoes, ever ready for worship. The family didn't own a television, and he wasn't allowed ordinary children's books. He also wasn't allowed friends over to play – in fact, he wasn't really allowed friends, because his parents, both communists, felt other children exhibited all the irreverence of those living hedonistic, capitalist lives.

'I think my blueprint was fairly clear. I was the only child in the parish who went to church every single day, where I was taught that any decisions I made today would impact not just my eternal life, but also the life of the whole world. I learnt that for my own mortal soul, and those around me, I had to do an examination of conscience before sleep each night. I also went to confession every week because I knew I'd done bad things and would go to hell if I didn't repent.'

What an enormous weight of expectation. Especially for a child. No wonder that by the time he was seven, Dominic walked around with a deep sense of unworthiness. Just imagine his horror when, a few years later and still a young boy who was attempting to be a saint, Dominic began to experience same-sex attraction. The only narrative he had ever received around homosexuality was that sodomites were on a mission to harm children and destroy families. Still, he couldn't help himself: every time he went to Bible class, he was drawn to a boy there. It was always someone with qualities that he felt he himself lacked, like confidence or an ability to make others laugh.

In time, the attraction to other boys intensified. He tried to hide it as best he could, but clearly his mother had sensed something. Her reaction, which was typically extreme, was to hand him a pile of pornographic magazines full of naked women having sex with men.

'I remember finding it really upsetting, seeing these women in the pictures and what they were doing. I wanted to cover their bodies up and help them to be happy because I thought they didn't look happy at all,' he told me.

When puberty arrived, things got worse. Dominic was appalled by the physical changes he saw in the mirror. The thought of inhabiting an adult male body was greatly stressful for him, but he also wanted to explore it, very much. The porn magazines he had been given were no help – they blurred out men's genitalia with the scornful message that you were 'looking in the wrong place' if you were interested in such things.

It was only in the changing rooms of the local swimming pool, where he now went alone to swim each week, that Dominic might catch a glimpse of what he was looking for. One day, when he was thirteen, a man got out of the pool alongside him and followed him to the changing room to watch him dress. No physical contact took place, however, until two years later. This time, a different man came out of a nearby shower naked, clearly aroused. Nobody else was around. The stranger approached Dominic with a lingering gaze. Dominic followed him into a cubicle.

'It was the first time I had experienced oral sex, and at the time it felt incredible. But immediately after, I was devastated and thought, *I'm going to go straight to hell*,' Dominic laments.

He went home, distraught. His mother could see her son was extremely upset but had no idea why. She called both a policeman and a priest and Dominic found himself confessing. He was told, in no uncertain terms, that what he had done was very sinful – he should repent and never let it happen again. The police also asked lots of questions, including whether he wished to press charges and then, when he declined, threatened Dominic himself with the charge of having sex in a public place. He might be underage right now, they said, but he certainly wouldn't be by the time the case got to court.

'I can't even describe the levels of shame and guilt. The priest may have given me absolution that evening, but I certainly did not feel forgiven. My mum was very angry. She held up a crucifix and said to me: *This is everything that is wrong [in the world] – sodomy! I knew you should never have worn that dress when you were little!* My dad never, ever talked about it at all, which was equally difficult – almost worse.'

There followed a series of similar sexual encounters with strangers in changing rooms. Each time, exactly as on that first occasion, Dominic enjoyed these short-lived connections, often experiencing them as quite profound. Afterwards, though, he was plunged even deeper into depression. When someone in the parish mentioned gay conversion therapy, Dominic felt a speck of hope. Maybe he could outrun his desire after all? If he just prayed hard enough, could things work out the way he wanted?

Dominic began to attend these secret meetings at least once a week. They were held discreetly in vestries and prayer rooms, organised by members of the church who employed various interventions, from psychodrama to prayer, to encourage participants to move beyond their 'perverted' homosexual desires and onto the one true path: of heterosexuality.

'Sometimes there would be a priest there, elaborating on the importance of chastity and celibacy or sometimes there was a speaker. Everyone was strongly encouraged to share very openly and bluntly about their struggles. We would act out very intense scenarios, often going back to traumatic events, like being bullied at school for being gay, and then re-working them in order to re-establish ourselves as heterosexual. But usually it just re-traumatised people.'

And yet Dominic continued to attend. What he truly longed for more than anything actually involved celibacy: he wanted to become a Catholic priest. But the Magisterium, Catechism and all the local church elders said that was impossible. Until he had sorted out his 'disordered inclinations', they insisted, he lacked the ability to relate to men and women: his vocation was out of reach.

Frustrated and confused, Dominic left home at eighteen to take an apprenticeship in London. He knew there was a strong queer community there and imagined a fresh start where he might be accepted into a different, more tolerant kind of family. It turned out, however, that the Catholic network was strong, with eyes and ears that extended all around the UK. There were people in London who were determined to stay close to Dominic. What began to emerge was a double life. On a Wednesday evening he would attend gay conversion therapy and then on Thursday head off for drinks in the gay enclave of Soho. On Saturday, Dominic would be standing with anti-gay protestors outside an LGBTQI+ friendly church, all of them expressing hatred and revulsion towards same-sex attraction. When the time came to leave, Dominic would walk away with the other protestors and, once he had said his goodbyes to them, he would double-back on himself, entering the very same church in search of support and understanding for his own same-sex attraction.

It was a disintegrated and lonely existence, one in which Dominic was constantly protecting his truest parts from view while also trying to fight for their survival. After three years, he took drastic action and went to live in a trailer on the outskirts of the city alongside hundreds of Irish Catholic Travellers. They were oblivious to Dominic's same-sex attraction, which was just as well since they had frequently been known to beat anyone they suspected of non-heterosexuality with baseball bats, leaving them for dead.

Yet still, Dominic chose to live there. It was an energetic place with few boundaries and much chaos, where dogs and children ran about as feral as one another. There was always a baby being born, a wedding taking place, someone drunk or bleeding somewhere. Mirroring this disorder was Dominic's inner sense of disarray – a man completely split and at war with himself; the part of him that wanted so much to be heterosexual enough to be deemed worthy of the priesthood and the part of him that had sexual needs and who so clearly desired men.

When crunch point came, Dominic was twenty-five and suicidal. He had all but destroyed himself with contrition. There wasn't a prayer or a pilgrimage he hadn't tried; he had spent days renouncing sleep, food or water; he'd been to all the shrines; he'd collected fifty different religious medals; he'd climbed barefoot in the holy town of Medjugorje and he'd gone on his knees around the statues in penance, skin ripped and bleeding. But wherever he went, Dominic met others who experienced same-sex attraction and were similarly unable to re-orientate themselves to the supposed *one true path*. Some of them had been trying for decades. They really could not have prayed harder.

Finally, almost exactly one decade after his first one, Dominic stopped going to the gay conversion meetings. The relief he felt was gargantuan. But there was grief in all this too: having lived his life thus far within the stronghold of organised religion made living the remainder without any kind of faith completely unthinkable. All that was left was his corporate office job, a vague faith in the divine and a group of Amazonian transwomen friends who supported and loved him with the kind of fierce maternal grace that he had so lacked as a young boy. He was desperate to believe in something – anything – that went beyond the tangible. But now there was almost too much choice available. And he did not know where to start.

So he began at the beginning, with the simplest of questions for himself:

What is it that I do believe?

And what is it that I don't?

What is it that I really think is true, and right and good?

And what do I know in my heart to be quite wrong?

Step by step, Dominic unravelled his entire life's tapestry and started again, threading himself together – a new picture.

'I still find boundaries hard. I struggle so much to say no when someone asks me to do something. I find it difficult to give myself enough rest and nourishment too. But at least now I can see that I have a choice, that I am choosing and have to keep choosing if I am to fight for the right to be my real self. So, if something doesn't speak to me, or makes me feel awful, I stop doing it. I have stopped going to confession, to Catholic conferences and Mass – things like that. Instead, I ask myself, *What do I really need, today?* This is about taking all the pressure away and just focusing on every moment, one moment at a time, and making nourishing choices for myself. Instead of worrying about whether I am going to hell, I try to think what I want for lunch.'

Sometimes a blueprint is virtually indelible, so shame-based and all pervasive that it can obscure choice, overshadowing it with thick lines of creed. Nobody will be able to refund this young man the hours spent twisting and tormenting himself in a bid to re-orientate to suit others. Yet his story is one both of cruelty and oppression *and* courage and liberation. It speaks of the psychic damage done when one is coerced, repeatedly, to contort oneself into the wrong shape, *and also* of the strength that can be found, eventually, to retaliate.

This retaliation is ongoing. In Dominic's case the critical voice of his church became his own, manifesting as perfectionism and, ultimately, self-abuse. This is a common result for those who have suffered abuse of any kind as children, where the initial crime becomes an 'inside job'; we internalise the abusive voice as our own as adults.

'I have this dream quite often that I'm being chased around the city, and I'm running as fast as I can, desperate and terrified. But I'm not fast enough, and I know it. I can't outrun this pursuer. At some point the figure that's hunting me down catches up with me, and I turn around to see who it is. And it's me. It's my face. I am the one chasing myself. I always wake up after that.'

What Is the (Your) Shadow?

'To become conscious of [the shadow] involves recognising the dark aspects of the personality as present and real. This act is the essential condition for any kind of self-knowledge.'

– Carl Jung

Dominic's story may be extreme, but it has universal elements, such as the damage done to any human being when their choices are reduced or denied by a wider group. Anyone who has traversed the sticky stage of adolescence, for example, must know how it feels to try to fit in. How many of us have grown up with parents who desperately wanted us to be more like them, say, rather than our truest selves? What about being an emotionally driven person born into a family of rational thinkers (or vice-versa)? How does it feel to have to exist within a system – political, socio-cultural or religious – that dictates how we should behave yet is at odds with our values or desires?

There are so many examples of the ways in which choices are limited by environment. Sometimes the most difficult part is undoing the damage done by all the internalised *shoulds* and *should nots* that we grew up with. One of the major things I've been championing in this book has been the process of bringing all these supposed rules to consciousness, particularly when it comes to how you relate to other people – your relationship, sex, intimacy and attachment blueprint. The point of this has been that when we a) notice we have a set of rules about this stuff we can then b) begin to wonder about what things might look like without such rules and c) get more choice-ist about it all and start deciding what actually works for us.

Sometimes these rules also come from us – the darker, unconscious aspects of ourselves that we can't or won't see. Things you'd look at and think, *That's not me!* are what Carl Jung called the psychological 'shadow'.

Interestingly, shadow material is often found in whatever we really detest about someone else: traits we say we'd *never* have. Where *always* and *never* goes, a shadow will probably follow. If I say I'm *never* mean, which is to say I'm *always* kind, then I probably refuse to see the times when I am mean and not kind. My meanness stays in the shadows, lurking, and my kindness is in the light, parading. In this instance, 'doing the shadow work' would involve recognising that on occasion I can, in fact, be mean. That meaner aspect of the self is no longer denied and no longer projected onto others. Instead, it becomes absorbed and tolerated. From there, it's a lot less damaging.

Returning to Dominic, his same-sex attraction was forced into the shadows, where it was hidden behind a curtain of shame and self-loathing. In the long run, this was unworkable, and repressing his desires for so long certainly had damaging consequences for his psyche. In that same story, there was the group of protestors who lined up outside the church to project their own internalised homophobia outwards, by instilling fear and damnation into the queer members of the congregation and all their supporters. This allowed their own same-sex attraction to stay in the shadows where it could stretch across others, darkening their light.

In Cassie's story (Chapter Five pages 103 and 115), Aidan denied his own neediness and instead projected it onto his loved ones. He would make flippant comments about the nature of his relationship to Cassie, like, 'For me, it's really just sex,' labelling her as the weaker, more emotional one. He would verbally deny his deeper need for connection and reassurance, and risk sabotaging relationships in order to stay in control.

The process of becoming conscious of the extent of their wounds and how they operated in their lives required Aidan and Cassie to sever their bond. Though that bond certainly included attraction and love, it was knitted together so tightly by their shared trauma that it proved incredibly difficult to unravel.*

* If this is something you'd like to explore more deeply, I suggest you investigate the term 'trauma bonding'. It is a phrase used by Patrick Carnes to indicate entanglement between individuals as a result of being devalued and rewarded repeatedly so as to set up a chemical bond between people. Nicole LePera, author of *How to Do the Work: Recognise Your Patterns, Heal from Your Past and Create Your Self*, defines this kind of 'trauma-bonded' relationship as one where there are cycles of emotional neglect, abuse, abandonment, violation of boundaries, controlling dynamics, enabling, shaming, push/pull or punishment dynamics. These kinds of relationships are particularly emotionally intense because they repeat our emotional wounding from childhood. That's why certain people end up in these dynamics where others would have left or never gone there.

Anita (from Chapter One, page 17) offers us an example of successful shadow work: what happens when someone owns their shadow material and is willing to bring it into the light. When her boyfriend Andrea began a new relationship with a younger woman she felt like she should be fine. After all, she had chosen to be non-monogamous. She tried to tell herself she was not allowed to be jealous, to push it firmly into the shadows, but this attempt at repression failed. It was more painful to deny her jealousy than to work through it. The truth is, when we try to stifle those big feelings, sooner or later they come back stronger and more damaging. The fact that Anita was willing to do this difficult, important work on her jealousy was one reason why she and Andrea were able to move through this challenging stage of their relationship.

Less Shadow = More Choice

For every unquestioned rule, there is an eerie silhouette. Whatever you feel you are *not* allowed has gone into the shadow. One cultural example is the prevalence of unconscious monogamy. If we are brought up to believe that we *must* be monogamous then we are more likely to project or act out any non-monogamous desires. Because we are 'not allowed' to have these feelings or instincts, we relegate them into the shameful shadows. Stuck there, they morph into destructive behaviours like illicit affairs or sexual repression, thus creating negative situations. Conversely, by shining a light on these feelings, they are less terrifying. Still scary, perhaps, but also known. To be consciously monogamous is to recognise, not repress or remove, all types of desire and to choose one partner because you *want* to, and not because you *have* to.

The key word here is *consciously*. True freedom, then, comes when we can embrace our shadow as a necessary part of the whole. It requires, more than anything, an ability to be curious rather than judgemental. Drop the black-and-white thinking about who you *should* be and think more about the kind of person you *could* be. There is a difference, after all, between aiming for the stars (healthy ambition) and insisting to yourself that you reach them (punitive dogmatism). If you *insist on* being always honest, you merely push dishonesty into the shadows. If you intend to be honest, and gently pick yourself up on the times when you aren't entirely truthful, you can stay on track more easily.

'Imperfectionism', as I like to call it, is the absolute key to fulfilling relationships. And, I might add, a fulfilling life. Contrary to popular, perfectionist belief, making progress requires us to embrace imperfection – not just our own, but other people's. There is something magical that happens in any relationship when we reclaim our shadowy aspects; we become less defensive and more able to admit to our flaws with a kind of, *Hey, I'm really sorry I did this, I guess I'm not always [kind, thoughtful, considerate – whichever] in the way I'd like to be or thought I was.* Sure, it requires vulnerability to be able to behave this way, but it is not usually as painful as suspected. People sometimes avoid admitting when they are wrong because they are scared the other person will 'use it against them', but in a healthy relationship vulnerability begets vulnerability; by bringing out softer sides we give the other person licence to do the same. Now you have two people who accept themselves as they are and try, from a place of greater wholeness, to do better. Progress, not perfection. Why can't we all just aim for that?

It isn't easy to take criticism. That's why so many people wander around with a long psychological shadow trailing behind them. For those who are able to continually reclaim their shadow – and it is an ongoing process – the rewards are great. Firstly, owning our shadow material helps us to take back projections, so that other people don't have to carry the burden of our own unconscious gunk. Secondly, as one old saying goes, *a bad day for the ego is a good day for the soul.* Owning up and meeting those unpleasant bits of you is great soul work because it knocks the ego off its perch as you begin to see you aren't quite as . . . insert whatever quality applies here . . . as you'd imagined. This brings the relief of humility, which leads to deeper compassion. 'Dare to be ordinary', as a wise teacher once told me.

'Sorry, not sorry' – *Vix's Story*

'When I talk to my non-disabled friends honestly about sex, suddenly I don't feel so alone. Turns out they are often going through something similar, and my disability isn't the only issue at all! Clearly, nobody talks about all this, so people have a positive perception of other people's relationships and negatively compare themselves. But that's wrong. We need to unlearn lots of our initial scripts around sex and just communicate the truth more.'

Vix is a twenty-nine-year-old activist with a degree in psychology. She has cerebral palsy, a complicated disability that can present with many physical and mental symptoms, and sometimes hardly at all. Vix falls somewhere in the middle, with limbs that feel like tin and a mind that could slice through iron. Her childhood was full of doctors, physiotherapists and operations. At nine years old, she underwent a particularly massive surgical procedure that required her to take a term off school to recuperate. The operation's goal was to improve her ability to walk and involved breaking and resituating both femurs and tibias, and stretching her Achilles tendon and hamstrings. Despite the success of this operation, Vix has used crutches ever since. Because her muscles are always tight everywhere, she suffers chronic daily pain.

The physical pain is the most severe, though the emotional pain comes close.

'When you see a four-year-old with splints on their feet or going around in a wheelchair, there's something cute that makes it palatable. But as a teenager, that stops happening. Puberty came, and all the usual things happened. I wanted to give off sex appeal but felt my body was mangled. I didn't have the cuteness of the disability anymore and I certainly didn't feel like I was beautiful. I started to spend ages choosing outfits. I'd go out wearing something I felt great in and would feel attractive for a moment. Then I'd catch myself in a shop window or something and I'd just emotionally crash. The way I moved, the shape of me . . . I never looked how I imagined. Reality devastated me.'

Vix had her first sexual relationship at sixteen. She dated the young man in question for six months, but neither of them made any reference to her disability – except once, when Vix's boyfriend made a passing comment about how his friend had asked what it was like to be in a relationship with someone disabled. She ended up in tears, saying, *Oh God I'm so sorry for having put you in that position.*

'I feel so sad now for that younger me who apologised for herself. But I felt like he was doing me some kind of favour by dating me. And when we had sex, I would just lie there thinking, *Really? Is this . . . it?* I was so used to not having access to things other people had, like the ability to walk down the street unaided . . . I think I just accepted this was my lot. Sex, for me, equalled pain.'

That relationship fizzled, but when another came along the situation was much the same. Different boy, same physical pain (Vix now knows this as vaginismus, a condition that makes sex very painful as it causes the vaginal muscles to contract involuntarily during penetration) and the same deep sense of unworthiness. More than anything, Vix didn't want sex to be yet another area of life in which she was supposedly abnormal. So she kept quiet about the pain and didn't explore what she might desire.

Thankfully, a couple of relationships down the line, things massively improved for Vix when she met her now-husband, P. It was loving and equal from the start, as P made it clear that passivity wasn't his bag; he wanted to do the things they could both enjoy because her pleasure gave him pleasure. P helped Vix to recognise that sex could be whatever they, as a couple, wanted. Though this has been both restorative and pleasurable for Vix, the pain remains. If she was offered a 'normal' body tomorrow, she would take it, she says, immediately.

'Yes, I still wish I wasn't disabled. It just really sucks on loads of levels. More than anything, though, it sucks because I don't have the same opportunities as other people. The lack of recognition of disabled people in our society means that I have absorbed the message that I don't deserve to take up space. Really, I just want to be allowed to live my life without unwanted commentary and supposed "help". I was coming out of a store yesterday, and a guy followed me all the way down the street, making comments about how I moved and how I walked. He got extremely close to me, ignoring my requests for him to please stop, telling me there was a centre in Hungary that would rehabilitate me if I visited. I told him four times to leave me alone before he did. I cried all afternoon after that – angry, frustrated tears.'

This is an example of the treatment that Vix has to deal with, but there are presumptuous responses too, like the taxi drivers who insist on putting down the ramp even though she explicitly says she doesn't need it. Or those who hand her prayer cards without warning. *Ask God for help,* they say. *He will assist you if you pray.*

Vix has a full collection of these prayer cards. Maybe she'll make an artwork from them one day. Or burn them instead. What she won't do any more, though, is placate others at her own expense. The impulse is first to make other people comfortable when interacting with her by making herself smaller or quieter. In order to go against this impulse and put her own rights and feelings first, Vix has to make conscious daily choices to take up space. Some days it feels exhausting, but it beats the alternative.

'Sometimes it feels like an uphill struggle, but if I don't make that choice every day to risk other people's discomfort, then nobody is going to examine their own prejudices about me and other disabled people. My condition was an accident of biology and, yes, I've found meaning in working as an activist so that all the little girls born [like me] tomorrow might not have to grow up in a world so unwilling to accept them.'

Choice and the Shadow – In Essence

'Shadow work' involves integrating the lesser-known parts of ourselves into our self-image to help us be authentically whole. To pull something out of the shadows could take years of introspection or a split second of insight.

Unconsciously, we push into that shadowy space the things we wish to hide from others and, where possible, also ourselves. Carl Jung believed that our shadow parts would show themselves via alternative means. These might include 'acting out', which is to express an emotion by a behaviour rather than communicating it, or 'projection' when we force that emotion onto someone else.

Remember that shadows and light go together. A shadow isn't the absence of light but a distortion of it. If you are wondering where to look to find some of your shadow material, the answer is: look closely at your light. Whatever you like about yourself and are happy to own is intrinsically linked to whatever you dislike about yourself and wish to disown.

Choice and the Shadow – Inquiry

The following questions are designed to help you nudge up against some of your shadow material. I've put example answers in italics.

1. Name one thing you were not allowed to do or be in the world in which you grew up? Write as much as you like about this idea, anything you notice.
   I was never allowed to show anger towards my mother. When she was angry with me she would show it sometimes by shouting but mostly by shutting down or going silent. I knew that if I was angry with her she would shut me out, so I made sure I was always nice to her because I really wanted her affection and love.

2. As an adult is there anything you find particularly difficult in close relationships?
   I find it really difficult to express anger when I feel it and I'm always scared that if I do, the other person will just leave the conversation, or the relationship. I really fear confrontation or disappointing the other person, so I squash my needs or upsets down until they end up coming out in a huge burst and causing damage.

3. Is there anything about yourself that you try to ignore and pretend isn't really there?
   If someone upsets or hurts me, I push it down because I feel like my feelings will probably be too much for them.

4. What qualities, behaviours and/or feelings do you show to the outside world? Think of how you would like your friends to describe you, the parts of yourself that you can happily identify with. (This relates to your persona.)
   Confident
   Warm
   Funny

5. Next, what qualities, behaviours and/or feelings do you prefer to hide from the outside world? Think of the things that a very close family member or a partner might have seen in you that you wish they hadn't or something you would rather keep hidden. (This relates to your shadow material.)
   Furious
   Repressed
   Timid

Take a look at those two lists. How much do you push that shadow stuff down? And what might happen if you shine more light on it? Would it become less scary and powerful? What do you fear people would say/do if they saw it?

Still feeling confused? Here's another good exercise. The next time someone really annoys you, ask yourself:

- *What aspect of my blueprint is this person denying?* You might think of this as whatever unwritten rule you have that this person is clearly breaking.
- *What freedom does this person give themselves that I do not give myself?*
- *Is this freedom something I might actually like? How might I allow myself more of it?*

Look at all the aspects of your relationship blueprint that you've identified so far. These are the things you've brought into the light. Now, imagine a shadow version in parallel. What shadows do these rules or structures create?

Now What?

Shadow work is about taking responsibility for your truth, first by figuring it out and then by sticking with it. It can be a shock to realise something about yourself that you genuinely did not know before. Once we see these things, we can't unsee them, so 'go gently', as one fabulous mentor of mine always used to say. This work is really like a snowball. Once you allow yourself to see or notice those things you have denied, momentum develops, and it becomes easier to roll with it. Let's take a broader look at society's shadows in the next chapter.

CHAPTER 8

SOCIETY AND THE SHADOW

Her Dark Materials – *Cath's Story**

> *'I think we need to know our inner darkness in order to have the choice not to act it out. What's definitely not choice is being controlled or manipulated by our shadow, because we are unconscious of it. If that darker stuff is not owned, then it is going to come out sideways. With the knowledge of who I really am, I have agency and free will. Now I really have some choice.'*

Cath sat on the bathroom floor, howling. She held her legs tight against her chest and pushed her forehead to her knees. The pain was insurmountable – inside her skull, her heart, her blood. Her mind said death itself would be relief. When would this awful suffering stop?

From the outside, all looked great. Cath lived in a beautiful house in rural Cornwall where she was a much-admired member of the community. Her business, offering therapeutic bodywork and massage, was really thriving. She was engaged to a lovely man and had a healthy teenage daughter. But nothing she saw or did felt real. She gave willingly to others, yet she felt empty. Life was like watching herself on tape – going through the motions, doing all the things that should make a person happy but never actually did.

This disconnect between what life looked like on the surface and what was really going on was familiar to Cath. She had spent her early childhood in a healing centre with practising spiritualist parents who were engaged in a toxic dynamic. Her father suffered from bipolar disorder and had been born into an addictive, incestuous family system. He consistently abused her mother, and she would pretend she was fine.

Eventually, they got divorced, but by then Cath had left home. Pursued by a constant sense of un-belonging, she had sought independence very young. In her early teens, she moved alone from the coast to Bristol, her family agreeing to grant Cath's request to fund a change of school systems so she could experience something bigger and more diverse. But even that felt too restrictive.

Cath quit school entirely and went to live in a squat with friends when she was fifteen. It was a happy few years, during which she both partied hard and trained as a holistic bodyworker. By the time she was nineteen, she had saved enough to go and live in Sydney, Australia, where she made money and friends with equal success. Here, in the early to mid nineties, she was also exposed to the gay scene in all its fabulous colour and verve. She met a woman who became her lover. It was a sensual and liberating time for Cath.

After two and a half years, Cath returned briefly to Bristol. Here she had what she calls a 'very difficult' relationship with an older man. After it ended, she decided to follow her mother to South Africa, who had a job out there. Cath partied hard again.

'After a series of really heavy nights out, I had a revelation and heard this inner voice saying, *You aren't going to be able to grow any more until you learn what it is not to be the centre of your own universe and have a child.* Within a week, I was pregnant. But it was the result of a rape. The man in question was HIV positive. It was a real crisis for me – the most awful thing that has happened to me and yet at the same time one of the most spiritual experiences I had, because in that moment my thought was, *I'm going to die, I'm going to die,* and I remember praying... *Give me this, child and save my life, and I'll do whatever it takes in order to support that being.* It might sound weird, but the whole room lit up, and I saw that soul land with me. I did not contract HIV but was left with the pregnancy.'

Cath returned to the UK to have her baby girl. All the partying, the drugs, drink, sex, wildness . . . it stopped completely. Here, she began her first period of celibacy as she attempted to work through the trauma of her rape and the period of depression that followed. She had a sense of constant searching both inside and outside herself for meaning. As part of this, Cath also moved through different kinds of relationships – non-monogamous, polyamorous, queer and heterosexual.

'It was like I was trying to crack the code, to work out what I needed. I can see now that I was also approaching my sexuality from a place that was more about self-protection. I found it easier to be in an open relationship because I felt nothing too deep was demanded of me. It's like I was tricking myself that I was exploring, but actually, I was hiding from some of my old wounds that needed to be worked through.'

Cath's final open relationship was the hardest, with double the pain and half the pleasure. There were jealousies on both sides and a distinct lack of boundaries or agreements. She had no big issue with her boyfriend's physical non-monogamy but struggled when he got emotionally close to other women. It was an interesting time, certainly, but also messy and volatile. So, Cath moved on from that to something new.

But still, those same wounds opened up. That's how she found herself, approaching her forties, unhappier than ever and slumped on that bathroom floor. In this moment, Cath saw with absolute clarity that something was very wrong. She couldn't continue like this, pretending she was fulfilled. She wanted to do something radical, to go away from everything. But if she did that, well . . . then what? She would do damage, not just to her community, her mother and partner, but most of all to her beloved daughter, who was now sixteen. Still, Cath's inner voice was very clear: *You have to leave this place or die.* Either she could abandon her child now and then return, more fully, later. Or she could stay, most likely take her own life and leave her daughter forever.

The next day Cath began to dismantle her life. She started selling everything she owned. She broke up with her fiancé and started an excruciating conversation with her daughter.

'Making that decision not to be a mother anymore was, without doubt, the hardest thing I've ever done. I told her why I had to leave and that she would be co-parented by her grandmother, though still financed by me. I tried to explain how this was part of a bigger, very conscious choice to place truth in the centre of my life, to get my head straight so that I could come back and be fully present in my life, as her mother and myself. She was distraught, but I knew I could not engage in relationships again until I had really taken ownership of some big shadow parts (particularly around historic father-daughter dynamics) that had shown up with lots of partners. Especially the last one. There were things I just knew I had to deal with, or I would be in pain forever.'

Cath left everything she knew, with no idea when she would return. First, she went to Denmark to spend some time with a renowned spiritual teacher who she believed could help her heal. After a few months, she moved to the Spanish wilderness, where she spent a year living off-grid in a state of self-enforced retreat. Here, she led a very simple life, with few distractions apart from chopping wood, carrying water, cooking, cleaning and her weekly trip to the local market where she would buy food and make one phone call home.

This was also the start of a five-year period of celibacy.

'Being away from all my responsibilities, in total isolation, was both blissful and really tough because everything I'd been hiding from emerged fully. I think I had to stretch out into the extremities of my experience and then sort of unwind, back to the beginning. But the trauma just kept unravelling. Like when you pull on a tiny thread, and it just keeps going and going.'

Slowly, though, things did improve. Two and a half years after leaving, Cath returned once again to the UK, no longer tormented by the shadows of her past. But what about her daughter? The separation had been brutal. Could their relationship now repair?

'Her fear of me leaving was ever-present, so when it actually happened it was her worst nightmare. But she got through it. The worst thing she could imagine actually happened *and* she survived. It helped her leave home and trust herself. Plus, I came back a much better mother – less haunted and more present. Those two things have helped her massively, though I would say it took us around two years to really repair the damage done by my leaving. Now our bond is at its strongest.'

When she returned, Cath was still celibate. During the ensuing two-year period, however, something very bizarre happened: she reconnected with all of her significant ex-lovers, bar one. Some contacted her directly, some serendipitously appeared, but each of them made it clear what they wanted: to be with Cath again.

'It was like the universe was offering me a choice,' she reflects. 'Like it was saying, "Hey, here are your foundational partners, all of whom have qualities that are important to you. What direction do you want to move in?" I followed my intuition, though, which told me to contact my first love, the only man that hadn't come after me. I was worried about disturbing his life, but it turned out he was single and living nearby. We met up and felt exactly the same as we had thirty years ago. Since then, we've been monogamous, which has felt really easy, and right! I think that, when it came to it, it was actually the deeper stuff in an intimate relationship that I really needed.'

Nobody said that choice was pretty. Sometimes we have to embrace exactly those things that we have learnt are ugly and wicked in order to also meet true beauty and goodness. Cath's story is one full of shadows – unconscious shadows that became known and then were faced, brought into the light – and might well invite judgement and criticism, particularly from those who query her choice to leave her child. But Cath is very clear on her reasoning and speaks freely about the dark side of motherhood: that paradoxical desire to both devote oneself fully to one's child, but also, sometimes, to be free of them.

It is often said that pain travels down the generations until one person is able and willing to feel it. In doing the work, that person starts to change life for themselves and their children. And their children's children, etc. It means they have unlocked the door to conscious choice and can do things differently, emancipating themselves and their offspring from the imprisonment of intergenerational trauma and stopping all the horrible crazy shit that just fucking hurts. Okay, maybe not all of it – that's a tall order – but some of it at least. It seems to me that, in abandoning her daughter, Cath also saved the two of them. Both truths can co-exist. Terror and freedom. Light and shadow.

Society and its Shadow

How can we make clear choices when we are living in society's shadow? Dominic and Vix from the previous chapter and Cath know about this struggle, but what about those who have a less extreme experience? The very existence of any cultural norm can make those who don't squarely fit it start to feel a bit *too* something. What if what we really want in life is just unusual? What if it's just not *the done thing*?

Age is a classic example of how society screws us all over. Just think of the insidious and damning messaging around what it means to get old and look old; how being over sixty, fifty (or even forty) *should* make us approach sex, or how we *should* tone ourselves down or be less appetite-driven as we age. But ageing doesn't always equate to maturity, for starters, and even if we do feel we've matured, why is that connected to a diminishment in desire or passion? Society's blueprint is that libido shrivels in conjunction with our skin – young people fuck all night, and old people caress one another before falling asleep in comfortable deckchairs. Such stereotypes are reductive, however much you enjoy deckchairs or all-nighters. The point is that we need to reconfigure the stultifying bits of our existing blueprint into something much lighter and more spacious.

Most reductive of all, perhaps, is the idea that older people – women in particular – should not express (or even have) any desire for sex. My friend Elaine has experienced this first-hand. When we met, I was twenty-nine, and she was sixty. We were both working as journalists and had the pleasure of enjoying a wonderful media trip to the Caribbean together where we mostly read books and sunbathed. She spoke freely about her enjoyment of sex, how consistent and fun sex was with her husband of thirty-two years before he died, and how she had continued to want and enjoy it since. She was quicker to dance and later to bed than those of us half her age because of her outlook: she never dismissed herself as being 'too old' for anything (nor any of us for being 'too young'), which at the time struck me as odd, though beautiful.

Elaine is now seventy-one, very single and very sexy. She is also a cancer survivor and a mother of adult children who lost their father twenty years ago. She is a very extroverted writer who loves socialising and has not yet considered retirement. There are so many ways I could categorise Elaine and never fully capture her essence. Despite this, her age seems to be all anyone notices – particularly those invisible men she would very much like to be dating.

'God, Lucy, I miss having a shag!' she tells me, sounding mildly frustrated. 'I so miss sex, and I so miss men! But dating is difficult for me. The main way of meeting people these days is over the internet, where age is one of the main filters. Also, people lie about their age on all of these apps, and I don't want to do that, so if I put seventy-one, chances are they'll think I'm seventy-five! I want a guy who appreciates me for who I am, and where my age doesn't make him feel sick. I know that can happen if someone meets me, but the problem is getting to that stage.'

Elaine is determinedly escaping 'the companionship straitjacket' – the notion that older people just want companionship and nothing else.

But because this straitjacket is societal, she's constantly fighting it off. So much so, in fact, that she's just emigrated to Seville in southern Spain, where it's hotter, more colourful and she feels less impeded by 'the very British Anglo-Saxon attitude that unless you are hippie or artistic you must outgrow your love of sex'.

'When I told friends in the UK that I still wanted sex it was as if I'd said I wanted to have sex with a dog! But not all women stop wanting sex after menopause. Why judge those of us who enjoy sex, orgasm and the physical presence of someone in their bed, or kitchen, living room or wherever, as the weird ones? I honestly don't know if I'll have sex again, as much as I'd like to. When I think about dying before my body is touched, or touches another body, in a sexual way again, I just feel really sad.'

Me too, Elaine, me too. And the words that come to mind when I sink into that sadness are *coercive de-sexualisation.* But how can we resist such a pernicious and powerful attitude? By defying the pressure to cover up or quieten down, both physically and sexually, and instead to do precisely what feels good for each of us. But it isn't necessarily as easy as simply being rebellious. Elaine's story – a woman discriminated against purely on the basis of her age – exemplifies how frustrating it can be to follow your heart and go against the cultural norm. Yes, we can all keep toeing the line and throw away our longings to enjoy the comfort of conforming – but at the expense of deep fulfilment.

If there were no *shoulds* left in the world, who could you let yourself be? You might feel uncomfortable, stepping out of the conventional way of doing things. But, then again, how uncomfortable is that straitjacket? The more I have broken away from any externally defined notion of how I should or shouldn't look, love or live, the less tension and anxiety I experience daily. Not to mention lots more joy. Uncovering what parts of your life are imposed on you and choosing instead to move passionately towards what you truly long for in your life – now *that*, to me, sounds like maturity. Deckchair or no deckchair.

Society and the Shadow – In Essence

The psychological shadow refers to all those parts of ourselves that we deny or just can't inhabit. The same principle can apply to family systems and communities, as well as a whole society. One example might be the family in which expressions of emotion are denied: if someone cries, nobody even acknowledges it; it is ignored. Or a leader engaging in illegal activity.

Society and the Shadow – Inquiry

1. Take a piece of paper, set a timer for ten minutes and write about all the ways in which you have tried to toe the line when it comes to being part of society. Try not to take your pen off the paper, even if it means filling in gaps with sudden thoughts about what you need to do today or how much you're hating this exercise. Ask questions like:
    - *In what areas of my life do I feel I've done what other people wanted me to do and in what areas have I not?*
    - *Why have I behaved this way?*
    - *Which of society's supposed rules have I ingested about the kind of person I should be? And which of those have cast a shadow? Who might I be without all that?*
    - *What does it mean to be different?*
    - *And, conversely, what does it mean to live a model life?*

What do you think is expected of you, and have you checked that out with other people? Even if they do agree that what you want is outside the realms of acceptability, do you care what others think? Worrying about how we might be seen is insidious in our society and leads to huge amounts of repression and misery.

2. Write a list of *shoulds*. Put in there all the things you think or feel you *should* be or do in your life. All those little comments in your

mind about what you should have done better today or should do differently tomorrow. Include all the massive criticisms and the most pernickety things you say to yourself, from *should have gone into the City* or *should never have got divorced* to *should have refused that doughnut at lunch* or *should have finished reading that novel.* Then write another list, with the why for every point. *Why* should(n't) you have done that? And then follow that answer up with another why. Do as many 'whys' as you need to drill down to where you get these ideas. Often when the answer is repeating it shows you've reached the end of the line with the whys. Now you can examine where this belief comes from, and whether it's time to retaliate.

Hopefully you can see in the example below – one from my own past – the way that subtle societal messages can contribute to daily self-bashing. In this example I use the idea that successful relationships are ones that never end – a common belief that can hold lots of people back from living their best life.

SHOULD	WHY	WHY	WHY	WHY	WHY
Should have tried harder to save my marriage.	Because a marriage ending = a bad thing and is a massive sign of personal failure.	Because when you get married it is forever. So success is staying together whatever.	Because that's what I've been taught to believe about relationship success.	Because that's still the prevailing view in much of our society. That's why we talk about 'failed marriage'.	Can't think of a good reason. Don't agree with this belief – I think I'll ditch it.

Now What?

Hopefully you've identified some of the ways in which you allow society's rules, explicit or not, to hold you back. But now what? It's not as if the *shoulds* we notice lurking in the shadows of our minds just disappear on spec because we spotted them. It takes time to resolve our *shoulds*, particularly if they are regularly reaffirmed or if you learnt them at a young, very impressionable age. Some of your self-negating beliefs may take decades to dissolve (as with Dominic's *I shouldn't be gay*) because they were instilled so forcefully. Others may be easier (*I should like running* or *I shouldn't need so much rest*), although they still need some unpicking. One of my main ones is: *I should be less sensitive.* Oh, I've been working with that one for years, and I can still go down that pathway a few times before I remember my promise to myself: to embrace my sensitivity as a gift and learn to take better care of it and myself.

Don't expect everyone around you to suddenly be supportive of your new outlook. It's wonderful if they are, but they are on their own journey, moving at their own speed. In extreme circumstances you might have to distance yourself from people who won't accept you as you are now, or perhaps you just need to set boundaries, e.g. *No, I'm not running any more because I've realised I don't enjoy it and I don't want to force myself to do it, so please stop trying to persuade me.*

Be patient but determined with both yourself and other people. Any *should*-based belief is likely to be rooted in fear, so imagine that you're talking to a scared child who needs convincing *that everything's okay.* They (that part of you) might not get it straight away; we're talking about thought paths in your mind that have become highways because of how many times you've gone down them. It takes some practice to re-route those thoughts, but I promise it's possible. Opening your mind in this way will also help you to communicate more constructively – an essential part of conscious relating, and also where we're going in the next chapter.

CHAPTER 9

CHOICE AND COMMUNICATION

A Tale of Two Marriages – *Rebecca's Story*

'In Ancient Rome whenever a General returned from battle victorious, he would be awarded with a triumph, rising in his chariot with laurels. But there was someone paid to stand behind him and whisper in his ear, remember you are mortal. This was to stop him becoming so full of his own grandeur and success that he overreached. I think there's a version of that story in my own. Five years ago, I was so excited by polyamory, the way you feel more love and really do experience more joy, maybe I thought I was a bit immortal. I prepared for all the logistical difficulties and jealousies. But I never prepared for the heartbreak.'

Rebecca was twenty-two when she met Andy, twenty-nine. It was back in the early noughties, when most people still stigmatised the idea of meeting someone via the internet. Rebecca wasn't worried about that: she just wanted to reassure herself, in the wake of a horrible break-up, that she'd still got it. Thankfully, there was chemistry and lots of it. The date went well, as did the many dates after that. Their interests were very different, but they clearly fancied one another, had great sex and loved each other's company. After just six weeks, they moved in together, because they both needed somewhere to live; Andy had just returned from travelling and Rebecca was moving towns to begin a postgraduate degree. Looking back, though, she sees the cost.

'Living with Andy from the get-go meant I didn't get to "do" my twenties in the way that people who aren't living with a partner do. I didn't get to sleep around and fall in love with inappropriate people. It was quite an ordinary relationship in lots of ways, and although I loved him, I grew dissatisfied. Because I come from a traditional background, I still pushed for marriage, to take that next step. But Andy resisted, which caused some issues because I felt he wasn't sure about committing and I was still missing out on other things since we were totally monogamous.'

Eight years into their relationship, Rebecca tried to break up with Andy. But during the same conversation, Andy proposed! Rebecca accepted his proposal, although she wasn't best pleased with how it had come about.

'I think I said something like, *I fucking knew you'd do this*! So now I feel like I've bullied you into this. And his response was, *I'm sorry, and yes, I know.* I told him to go away and come back and do it properly. We went on holiday to Greece, he had bought a ring . . . and he suddenly stopped me on the way to the loo to ask me to marry him . . . I was like, um, yes, but I need to wee . . .' She laughs and continues: 'So it wasn't the most romantic proposal at any point. But it stepped things up a notch.'

Being legally bound to each other solidified them. It made them sort issues out more quickly and with more commitment. But then, a few months after their honeymoon, Rebecca and Andy looked at each other and thought *what now?* Neither of them wanted kids at that stage. Was romantic life going to just carry on this way forever?

At the time, Rebecca, who works in the theatre, was collaborating on a show about desire. She was working with a kindred spirit who was also a relationship anarchist. They had interesting conversations that opened her mind to other non-monogamous, non-conformist ways of loving. Rebecca's perspective widened, and she knew that it could never again narrow. Soon afterwards, sitting on the sofa, hand in hand with her husband, she started a conversation about opening up their marriage.

It wasn't an easy moment. At first, Andy was hurt. He seemed quite scared. But he was willing and open-minded. They attended a polyamory meet-up at the Central London café Coffee, Cake & Kisses. Rebecca and Andy liked what they saw and heard, and a month or so later they took what Rebecca calls the 'original holy-fuck moment' and went on dates with other people.

In the back of their minds, they both worried: was this the beginning of the end? Or was it just the beginning of something new?

For Rebecca, at least, it was an important stage, which changed her relationship with herself: 'I'm a fat, kinky, bisexual, forthright woman so for my whole life I have been taught, explicitly or implicitly, that I should consider myself lucky to get anything sexually or romantically . . . Turns out that I exist at an intersection of niche tastes, and for a significant proportion of people out there I'm the fucking holy grail! Who knew? Sleeping with other people gave me the chance to be "the hot girl" for the first time in my life. It was absolutely great and meant that I returned to my relationship with Andy with swagger and confidence – he loved it.'

They both discovered there was something rather galvanising about having one-night stands or flings with other people and yet still wanting, most fundamentally, to come back home to one another ('It was like a palate cleanser,' says Rebecca). Now they could freely choose to still have sex with one another, rather than doing so simply because they were each other's only ethical sexual option. There were definitely teething issues, though. Despite the rules the couple had initially put in place – *please, not in our bed* and *always come home when you say you will* and *no sex with anyone in our friendship circle* – insecurities sometimes took over and screw-ups were made, like the time they threw a party and Andy walked in on Rebecca and her boyfriend doing a whole lot more than chatting . . . Thankfully, however, given their pre-existing intimacy and commitment, they were able to talk about anything and come out of each upset stronger than ever. The things they have had to address in order to live the way they do means they are more, not less, honest and connected. And trust has amplified.

Almost exactly a year after opening up their marriage, things took a turn in a new direction as Rebecca met J, who became a serious boyfriend and one of the great loves of her life. He was very different to Andy in many ways – their relationship included much more intellectual argument and power play, for example – but also felt familiar to Rebecca in the same way her husband did. Having a relationship with both men simultaneously allowed Rebecca to access wildly different parts of herself on any given day. It was a very happy time. As a result, Rebecca wanted to be completely honest with everyone about their love lives. Andy preferred to keep things private, though. He was extremely supportive in the face of Rebecca's family's reaction to the news – a tirade about how Rebecca's polyamory was akin to prostitution and her marriage no longer 'proper' – but still Rebecca felt resentful that he self-censored around his own family and friends.

Three years after it began, Rebecca and J's relationship broke down irrevocably. This loss was devastating for Rebecca, who fell into an extended period of depression, during which she was so overwhelmed by heartbreak that she was unable to give her marriage anything close to the emotional energy it required. More problematic was that Andy witnessed her desolation. For a spouse to support someone in such deep grief over someone else was, Rebecca admits, 'a whole new level of insanity and agony, which wasn't good for anyone'. It also points to one of the most complicated and poignant things about any kind of consensual non-monogamy: watching someone you love grieving another relationship. All while you stand in front of them with arms open, wondering why your presence hardly helps.

It took eighteen months, but eventually Rebecca moved on from her heartbreak. When she emerged, Andy was there, though now it was he who was harbouring resentment, having felt hurt by Rebecca's recent neglect of their marriage even though he knew, logically, she couldn't help it. It was around this time that Andy met V, the first woman during this period of non-monogamy with whom he found a deep and important connection. This was tricky for Rebecca.

'I'd had five years of being the person mostly out and about in a poly relationship, and he'd been the one mostly at home. I expected him to give me the same level of care as I had when we were starting out on all this because I hadn't relaxed into him being out so much yet. But he assumed that we were both old hat at all of it. And it was this misunderstanding that caused a difficult period, not so much me having an issue with Andy loving someone else. So it isn't as much about things being equal, but more about them being equitable.'

Then came a global pandemic, and some fresh conversations about having children. Given all the restrictions around socialising and physical contact, it seemed an obvious time for Rebecca and Andy to invest in themselves as a couple, and Rebecca, at least, assumed that if a baby was born there would be little time for another serious love affair for two or three years, minimum. Andy, however, had other ideas. He really loved V, he explained to his wife, and he wanted to continue seeing her after the pandemic eased, regardless of whether he became a father. Time for more very difficult conversations and some epic rows as those buried resentments emerged.

'Navigating this latest change has been hard labour,' admits Rebecca. 'There have absolutely been times when I've thought, *Why am I doing this? Let's jack it in.* I think I was shrinking my world and nesting in preparation for having kids and it felt like his response was just to go and fall in love with someone else for the first time. I wasn't sure I was happy to step up to the challenges of having poly relationships whilst also giving my entire bodily autonomy to having a child. For a while I wondered if I still wanted it – if polyamory was worth the cost.'

There were other reasons, too, beyond the relinquishing of her body and time, that made Rebecca fearful of entering parenthood on anything but the most solid of footings. Strangely, these were similar to the reasons why she was attracted to polyamory in the first place. Rebecca's own parents' marriage was the product of an illicit affair, and her father went on to have more clandestine relationships, to which her mother never consented but always knew about.

'I think one of the reasons I'm polyamorous is that I see that tendency [to want more than just one lover] in myself and I don't want to be an arsehole. There were certainly times before we opened up our relationship when I fantasised about having an affair and had we continued being monogamous, I may well have ended up doing it and then come home and lied about it. That would have been so destructive – to us and to me. Who wants to pretend to be someone else in their own life? Not me. It's horrible. Now there isn't anything I lie about, which means that whoever is spending time with me gets the real me, 100 per cent.'

The real me, 100 per cent. Rebecca's words really made me consider: how many of us are that genuine? In what ways do I hide parts of myself? What am I not communicating that prohibits me from being faithful to who I really am?

I could think of a few things. More, honestly, than I was proud of. It made so much sense to me that, for Rebecca, who grew up around lies and unspoken betrayal, being transparent is essential. Actually, life-affirming. In order to do that, she has to communicate constructively, with a focus on building intimate understanding. The section below looks at some of the pillars of this kind of progressive communication, and how to cultivate it in your relationships.

Constructive Communication

What makes communication constructive, rather than destructive?

When people talk about wanting someone to communicate more with them, what they really mean is that they want that person to communicate more constructively. We often just don't communicate what we want to communicate in the way we want to communicate it!

When I write about communication here, I'm fundamentally talking about emotional communication, about deeper things, rather than how you ask someone to pick up a pint of milk at the supermarket for you. The word 'communication' comes from the Latin word *communis,* meaning 'to share or impart' something, with connotations of an exchange. This section is designed to help get you thinking about the various ways in which you share and express yourself, deliberately or not, so that you can recognise your patterns and, if necessary, think about change. Some of your communication methods may work well for you, but others not so much. Rage, for example, even when it decimates any chance of resolution, still communicates something important, like the presence of hurt and dysregulation. Silence communicates too but is every bit as destructive as rage because it is invalidating to both parties and entirely prohibits a dialogue. Evasion is a form of communication. As is blame or withdrawal. These are actually very effective ways of communicating – who doesn't pay more attention when someone screams at them or ignores them? – but they are in no way constructive.

For communication to be truly constructive, therefore, it must be honest and considered. It all begins and ends with your willingness: the willingness to hear and speak the truth. There are plenty of skills we can teach or learn, all of which can enhance our communication no end, but if we are not willing to brave the truth then we will never communicate constructively about anything emotional. At its most fundamental, constructive communication involves being oneself; being able to express well what you do or don't want. As Rebecca said so succinctly: 'Who wants to pretend to be someone else in their own life? That's just rubbish.'

Being fully ourselves, being *vulnerable*, can be daunting. Sometimes we are so hell-bent on keeping the peace with others that we end up abandoning ourselves and our own needs. Communicating constructively with people you value and care about will always involve some degree of vulnerability as you override any desire to self-protect, particularly during or after a conflict. It can feel hard but stick with it and you'll be grateful. Breaking through those barriers to constructive communication can really improve your relationships and increase your self-worth.

The more we get to know our every quirk, the more we open the door to transformative relationships. Learning to communicate well is a bit like playing an instrument – you can have the best technique in the world and practise for forty hours a week, but if you've no musicality, you'll never be great. Similarly, you can have all the communication skills nailed, but if you aren't speaking from a truthful place inside, then something about what you're saying just . . . won't . . . quite . . . land.

Tips for Effective, Authentic Communication

How do we move towards authentic communication and expressing ourselves fully? There are many books that cover this subject comprehensively, but the most beautiful I've read is David Richo's *How to Be an Adult in Relationships.* Likening the process of maturation to a heroic journey, Richo makes it clear that communicating oneself authentically is an integral and extensive part of emotional maturity – a task that requires far more than the mere decision to do so. We must become acquainted with any old wounds and the ways we have adapted in order to self-protect from any re-wounding before we can create space to react in different ways to any triggers that may arise. Only once we understand ourselves well enough can we begin to take risks in, and responsibility for, the way we communicate with others. Now, we're really talking. And from a conscious, non-aggressive place. Here are some tips for improving communication with those important people in your life.

Create a safe container: Don't the most important things in life deserve some preparation? Establishing the right conditions for a DMC – a deep-and-meaningful conversation – gives you the best chance of successfully connecting. Do you have enough uninterrupted time? It doesn't have to be the perfect amount, but if you have guests coming in five minutes, is it wise to begin right now? Are you even looking at one another? Is there the physical space to talk or are the kids also in the kitchen? Launching into a monologue when you're hoping to arrive at a dialogue isn't ideal; we do better to start an important conversation with a little caution. Catching people off-guard like this can really increase the chances of getting a negative or defensive reaction. That's why just kicking off with something like, *Hey, I want to talk to you about something important; are you available right now?* gives you a chance to avoid a potentially hurtful response and gives them the opportunity to get into the best mindset so that they can really hear you. This way, they can also take better care of your feelings if they don't want to talk right now, by saying something like, *Yes, I want to listen but after I've finished sending this email,* or *I'm feeling really anxious now – can we talk later when I'm calmer?*

Taking a few basic steps to create the best conditions for constructive communication can make all the difference. It can be useful to put a boundary around how long you'll talk about a specific subject (more manageable = less anxiety-inducing) and then set a time to revisit it if it's not sorted out. It's okay to leave things midway, so long as you know when you'll return to it.

Listen: *Really listen, with your head and heart* to what someone is saying *and* how they are saying it. Listen for the sake of listening and not because you want to respond in a certain way or are trying to make someone feel better. Yes, you might receive answers to questions, and you might make someone feel better, but that's not the deeper purpose here. Listening for its own sake is enough. It is an act of love – a consensual surrendering of self, in service of the other. The longer I work as a therapist (and have therapy myself), the more I think that at least 80 per cent of its positive capacity comes down to the therapist's embodied receptivity; their ability to be physically, mentally, emotionally present and receive what is being communicated. It sounds basic because it is, but it is also the most demanding part of the job, to sit in a chair and really listen to the person before us. This isn't done to facilitate extreme self-obsession in the person receiving therapy, but to help them achieve a greater level of consciousness. This enables them to go about their life with more freedom and compassion, not just for themselves, but for others, *precisely because they were truly seen and heard.* The songwriter Dar Williams puts it perfectly:

> And when I talk about therapy, I know what people think,
> That it only makes you selfish and in love with your shrink,
> But oh, how I loved everyone else,
> When I finally got to talk so much about myself.
> – 'What Do You Hear in These Sounds'

I am absolutely not suggesting that you take on the role of therapist for anyone! It's not a healthy dynamic to get into and not your job. What I'm suggesting is that you practise wholehearted listening for periods of time. Try it, for fifteen minutes; really focus on who you're with. Ask yourself what you notice when they talk? Listen to their words *and* their silence. "Listen" to their body: observe how they are moving, how they hold themselves, and be aware of your own internal responses, as those can offer big clues as to what's going on as well. There is such simple magic in this. It is also, perhaps, the most loving thing we can do for someone. Just to really, really *listen.* So much more loving, I think, than offering advice or trying to push them towards solutions.

Speak about your thought processes, not your mind: People talk about "speaking their mind", but try speaking your thoughts and feelings instead. Good communication involves helping someone else to understand where you are coming from. Showing someone else what's behind your behaviour or decisions is the best way of helping them understand you, particularly when it comes to communicating intimately through conflict. From that place of understanding, hurt will probably reduce.

For example, saying, *Sorry, I'm stressed, need space, let's reschedule,* is one way of communicating, but it's nowhere near as constructive as explaining considerately where you're coming from, saying something like: *I'm really nervous about saying this to you because I don't want to hurt your feelings, but I'm so stressed, and I just need some time for myself this week. Can we just see each other at the weekend, when I've had space?* Taking the time to word things well so that the emotion, not just the upshot, is conveyed, can make all the difference, particularly for partners with an insecure attachment (page 111).

Develop body awareness: Learning to understand the way your body communicates your feelings to you is an extremely valuable use of time for anyone who wants to understand themselves better and have high-quality relationships with others. It is a vast and deep subject, well worth exploring in more depth (Suggested Further Reading, page 223). In this short section, however, I'll offer a sense of why and how the body can communicate, expose or even betray what we're feeling. Thinking about emotions in a way that pays attention to the sensations that accompany or even precede them can be extremely helpful, not just in enabling you to name for yourself, and another, what is going on, but also in containing it a little. Think of a restless foot. It keeps on jiggling even though the person to whom it belongs insists they have nothing to communicate in words. What is that foot trying to communicate? What might it say that isn't being spoken? Our intuitive reactions to stimuli inform what we may think about a situation. If we listen to our bodies, we can authentically communicate our feelings to each other and, more importantly, ourselves. Ask yourself: what is my body communicating with this sensation? What is it telling me that I need?

Obstructions to Effective, Authentic Communication

In the same way that we can support ourselves to communicate more constructively, we can also obstruct our progress. The obvious blockers to satisfying self-expression include things like *not* listening fully, *not* sharing how your mind works and *not* becoming interested in the wisdom of your body and its somatic responses in life.

The following list covers some of the less obvious ways in which we might sabotage or miss out on effective, honest communication. This can include the things we do deliberately, maybe out of fear, as well as the things we do without realising, often as a result of the *shoulds* and *shouldn'ts* that we've inherited or been taught.

Rushing

Do you know what you're trying to communicate? Have you had enough space and time to really think about what it is you want to get across? Rushing is probably my own biggest communication blocker. When things are going well, and I feel tuned in to myself, I can communicate my truth fast and considerately. But when I'm stressed or upset, I need to take much more time to delve into what's going on before communicating it to the relevant person. Sometimes that means putting off a conversation until I'm ready. Not indefinitely, but just until I can get some clarity around the situation. I've learnt that *I'll need to take some time to think about that and get back to you* is a viable response to an important or challenging question either from someone else or from inside your own mind. It's impossible to communicate very constructively when you are flooded with pure emotion or confused about what you're trying to say. Taking time to soothe myself with things like yoga, meditation, speaking to my therapist or trusted friends, writing or sketching things out helps me figure out what I'm feeling and why. Then and only then can I communicate constructively.

Mind-reading

Exposing the workings of your mind – the twists and turns it takes – is so much better than expecting someone else to just 'get it'. Mind reading, by which I mean assuming or guessing what's going on inside another person's mind (or expecting them to know exactly what's going on in yours), is the fastest route to confusion. I can pinpoint at least one romantic relationship and a couple of important friendships that I've lost precisely because of this communication blocker. Despite its havoc-wreaking properties, adopting the position of mind reader or mind readee is all too common; the more intimate we are with someone, the more we might expect them to always 'get' us. Maybe that's because when someone does read us correctly in that way, it can feel blissful. But the truth is, however well someone knows you and your mindscape, they still aren't in it! So, instead of thinking, *I shouldn't have to explain that, they know what I'm saying really when I say, 'I don't care',* try to communicate clearly. It's dangerous to go through life expecting any other human being to fill in the gaps in your communication. The more we can narrow those gaps, the better.

Communicating to control

You know when you approach a conversation with a clear idea of how you want the other person to react or respond? When you choose your words oh-so-carefully in the hope that you can encourage them to feel or think a certain way about what you're saying? I doubt there is an adult in the world who hasn't done this but noticing and swerving round it is an excellent communication goal. Trying to direct a conversation is controlling – just another kind of avoidance as you attempt to keep an interaction within a specific frame that suits you. We don't have the right to try to control another person. The most constructive thing you can do is to work on sharing yourself as mindfully as possible and then listening to the response as fully as you can. You might be surprised about the direction things take when you communicate with less of an agenda.

Communicating in chaos

It's difficult to communicate constructively if you are flooded with stress. When internally dysregulated, it's common to choose the wrong words, babble or freeze, and start denying or abandoning your (or the other person's) needs. Whether you fly upwards towards panic or sink downwards towards dissociation, heading out of your comfort zone will negatively impact your ability to communicate well. If you know you're about to have a potentially inflammatory conversation with a partner, for example, decide beforehand on a signal or word that indicates the need to take time out if you're getting really upset or zoned out. It is okay to lose your shit sometimes (hello, human), but it's also very hard to communicate well from that lost place. Take time to come back to yourself before you start again, not because you don't care about the conversation but because you care enough to do it justice. The best communicators aren't those who can ignore dysregulation, but those who can notice it and pause, taking the steps they need to reorient themselves towards a sense of inner balance.

The one-shot attitude

So, you've decided to take a risk and communicate something potentially tricky to a loved one. You take a deep breath, say what you need to say, and the whole thing goes down a path you didn't expect or want. Maybe the other person gets defensive. Perhaps your words came out all wrong. Maybe you saw something in their face and then clammed up. Now you wish you'd never started. Argh! You feel even worse. *Please remind me never to try constructive communication again,* you think. *I should have just kept myself hidden.*

Believe me, I empathise. When I come forward and show myself in those moments of defencelessness, I really need the other person to get it. When they don't, I feel like I have fallen down a massive black hole that's too dark for me to escape. My first reaction, even after all these years of therapeutic work, is to withdraw like a snail into her shell. But if there's anything that this work has taught me, it is that we can always do things differently, even after we've done them the same way we always did! So, hours or sometimes days after my withdrawal, I'll give it all another shot. After all, why would I give someone I really care about just one chance at understanding? If it keeps going wrong, maybe now really isn't the right time. If that person doesn't want to, or can't, understand what I'm trying to communicate, perhaps I need to reassess what it is I'm trying to say, or whether they are able to receive it. And if they aren't, what does that mean? Perhaps this calls for a deeper inquiry into the relationship itself and whether it's working for both of you.

Communication and Conflict

Even the best communicators in the world can't insure themselves against conflict. Good job, because locking horns with another can be pretty affirming when it's done right. Choose to ignore enough important issues in a relationship and you will eventually lose touch with its beating heart and perhaps also with yourself. How can you know what really matters to you if you don't fight for it sometimes? How do you know your feelings count if you aren't prepared to voice them under pressure? If we are unwilling to engage in the occasional conflict, then either we become just background noise in our relationship or the relationship becomes just background noise in our own lives.

Some kinds of conflict are destructive, like vicious late-night arguments supposedly 'forgotten about' the next morning. Other kinds of conflict can be more positive, helping to forge bonds and deepen trust in another person. What relationship doesn't strengthen, for example, when two people value and respect each other despite having different views? It's easy to enjoy the company of someone who shares your tastes but to relish having a relationship with someone who challenges you offers an entirely different, more nuanced flavour.

So why then, given all its potential to incite breakthroughs in communication, does conflict have such a bad reputation? Why do so many of us fear it? I've met skydivers and ultramarathoners – people clearly not averse to a little physical discomfort – who'll go out of their way to avoid any kind of disagreement. Perhaps they were told that only bad children made a fuss. Or they were stuck between warring parents, for whom fighting was like a game with no clear end. Maybe they were taught that letting other people's bad behaviour go made them the better person – the nicer one. Or maybe conflict meant being left: if they disagreed they were abandoned, emotionally or physically.

If anything like this informed your conflict resolution, then it's no wonder you avoid it. Taking a less defensive stance and opening yourself up to the possibility of healthy conflict will likely improve the quality of all your relationships. Rebecca and Andy managed this and reaped the benefits. They learnt, through butting heads and making mistakes, that in order to work through conflict well they needed an understanding of each other's history. Rebecca realised that Andy is not demonstrative, either in how he fights or how he loves. She knows that this comes from the way he grew up, in a family where expressions of love, physical or emotional, were rare, if not extinct. Rebecca was the first person in Andy's life to ever tell him she loved him, for example. Andy knows that Rebecca's family was the opposite. Their home was full of loving words, arguments and emotional outbursts, albeit without much resolution. Given all that, it makes more sense to both of them that their responses to conflict are very different. Andy's is to dig in and keep still. Rebecca talks about how difficult this can feel, and how they have learnt to deal with it.

'He goes all armadillo, and I'm like a terrier. We've learnt not to judge each other, but just to accept that we process emotion in totally different ways, good and bad. If I feel something, I react! Andy doesn't do that, though, so I have to have faith that he feels stuff because it doesn't always look like it. And he has to have faith that when I'm freaking out it isn't the end of the world. It's just that our calibrations are different.'

Communication, for these two, is an education. They've developed techniques, like holding hands during a conflict, that help them move through the tricky moments. Maintaining a physical connection helps to modify emotions, even when the tone of their words gets harsh. They also have a rule about putting phones away when they haven't seen each other properly in a few days. 'It's easy in that period when you've had supper together and are watching a box set to be on your phone to someone else – someone new and fun in the poly world.' And then there's scheduling, with spreadsheets! Rebecca and Andy have realised that if they don't look at their diaries together, and plan their weeknights ahead of time, then their priorities can go haywire. 'This week, we wrote down what was going on for both of us and realised that the only night we had together was Monday. Was that enough, really? I mean, isn't this relationship the thing that is supposed to be at the centre of our life? *No*, we thought, *no*, and because we could see it in black and white, we had to admit it and correct it.'

Whether or not this couple will become parents remains uncertain, although the conversation remains very much open, as does their relationship. Having come through a difficult stage in the last eighteen months, things are still 'crunchy', according to Rebecca, and both are wary of screwing up. They are just as committed to the relationship, though now with even more commitment to their personal needs.

'What I've realised through feeling resentful or annoyed is that sometimes what I communicate to Andy, I can also communicate to myself. So, like, if I'm feeling he *shouldn't* be doing something, then maybe I can avoid saying, *Please don't do that thing that you're obviously doing to make yourself happy,* and instead just step up and do more of whatever it is that I need to be happy – the thing I want to do.'

Two's Company, Three's Allowed – *Maggie, Cody and Janie's Story*

> *'When I met Cody, we quickly became like an old married couple. When I met Janie, we quickly became like old friends. But now we're just an old married throuple! The triad is the unit. It's our base – it's ground zero.'* (Maggie)

In the attractive enclave of Redbank, a small, hip suburb surrounded by the American city of Chattanooga, three lovers are happily renovating their future home. It is currently uninhabitable – more like a shell than a house: missing walls, windows, doors and floors. There aren't any functioning electrics or plumbing yet either, but these three aren't worried. They know, from their relationship history, what it's like to build something from the ground up. Something truly bespoke.

It all began seven years ago when Maggie met Cody on Tinder. Cody was twenty-six at the time, Florida-born, from a white-picket-fence family with married parents and two siblings. He had just come out of a relationship and wasn't looking for another, but when he met Maggie, a fiery twenty-two-year-old from California, his heart immediately expanded. Their first meeting was a coffee, but the connection was obvious and strong. Very quickly, they fell in love in a committed and serious way, discussing marriage on the third date. Monogamy just sort of . . . happened, until, about four months into their relationship, they overheard Cody's flatmate having a threesome. This made them giggle and got them talking . . . Was it something they, too, wanted to do? Maggie was bisexual, after all, and Cody curious. They felt entirely secure with each other, so why not explore a little together?

Within a week Cody and Maggie had set up a joint profile on Feeld, the sex-positive dating app designed for both couples and singles. They enjoyed a few casual hook-ups without incident. A few months later they met twenty-one-year-old New Yorker Janie – another hook-up, they assumed. But after drinks, chat, sex and more chat, Maggie texted Janie: *Shall we all meet up again?* What started out as purely sexual moved into sex and friendship. Then, as the friendship deepened, the nature of their triad morphed again, towards romance. Now they also cuddled, cooked, watched TV, laughed or went out rock-climbing together. It all felt good, so they kept doing it. They let things change and change again.

Nine months passed and Maggie and Cody were still meeting with Janie regularly. Sometimes it was the three of them and sometimes, when one was out of town, just two would meet. When Maggie and Cody decided to go ahead and get married, for both financial and romantic reasons, they picked Janie as their Maid of Honour. Something about this change in status encouraged Cody and Maggie to discuss again whether they wanted to move forward with their married lives with Janie so closely involved. The answer was a resounding *yes.* Her enthusiasm and support, happily playing such an important role in their big day, also solidified the bond between the three of them. When the day came, they didn't officially come out to any of the guests as polyamorous, but nor did they try to hide it. Not only was Janie virtually the only non-family member present at the tiny ceremony, but also, as soon as the bride and groom had finished their traditional first dance, Cody grabbed Janie's hand and started dancing with her.

Husband, wife, girlfriend. It was a marriage made in heaven.

Until it wasn't, of course. Nothing stays the same forever. But could they roll with the changes or not? A few months passed and now Janie was upset. Her feelings were growing, and yet their set-up hadn't changed. There were still so many people who didn't *know,* and Maggie and Cody, as the original romantic unit, seemed to have the final say in things. It felt to Janie like it was them (two) plus her (one), rather than all of them (three), and it no longer felt okay.

She wanted to address it but didn't know how. The feelings rose inside her until they spilled right over. Tearful and angry, she told them both she was deeply in love with them and wanted more, much more, than to simply be an extension of their couple. Why wasn't this reflected in their setup? It really hurt, she realised in speaking, to be the extra one rather than an equally central part. Maggie and Cody agreed: they both felt the same. Something had changed between them, in their dynamic. Now they had seen it and named it, the way they lived had to change too. No more avoidance of the truth, they all decided. It was time to live their lives like a real 'throuple'.

That was the theory, but what about practice? None of them knew what living like a throuple really meant or how to explain it to their nearest and dearest. Maggie's family were fairly liberal and Cody's family just a little less so. For Janie, however, it was complicated, having grown up in the Apostolic Pentecostal Church – she left at eighteen – that strictly disallowed anything that was not heterosexual and monogamous. Also, the women within the community were not allowed to cut their hair, wear make-up or trousers, or dress 'immodestly' . . . You can probably imagine how bisexuality and polyamory went down. Nonetheless, Janie wanted her family to know the truth, so she asked her cousin to tell her mother: your daughter is in love with two people, one woman and one man, and now they are all in a throuple together.

What came back wasn't awful. Janie's mother made it clear that her love was the same, if not greater, than ever. *Although I don't agree with or condone your choices,* she added, which stung.

'It's hardly a choice, though, is it, being bisexual?' Janie baulks. 'Is it that much easier, pretending to be straight?'

As part of this shift towards equality and authenticity, Cody and Maggie invited Janie to move in. The plan was always to buy somewhere together, in equal shares, but first they had to save. As time went on, their families began to embrace the new throuple even if they didn't always understand it. They all spent Thanksgiving with Cody's family and Christmas with Maggie's, where there were presents and love for each of them.

So far so good, but not everything was so easily adaptable for the new throuple. Think about all the things that are set up for two in our society. Booking a table for three is no problem, but hotel rooms and holidays aren't so easy. Much more seriously, if something were to happen health-wise to Janie, neither Cody nor Maggie would automatically be informed. But that's just like any other romantic partner of a patient, right? Not really, no. Since they are married to one another, the law won't ever recognise them as Janie's partners, so if Janie was seriously ill in hospital, it would be entirely legal for the doctor to tell them nothing. Cody and Maggie would be left outside the hospital door, relying on their partner's family in New York.

The greatest challenge these three faced, however, came from within, not outside, their triad. The 'dark days' arrived about a year after Janie moved in. Months of destructive communication meant that the relationship between Janie and Maggie, which had never been quite as straightforward as the other relationships in the triad, was crumbling. Sex became a pivotal issue as the two women struggled to deal with their mismatched libidos. They said 'real mean girl shit' to each other via snide comments and passive aggression. Both women were too stubborn to give up, but also too full of anger to continue in any remotely healthy way. And Cody was in the middle, full of frustration and despair. The way they saw it, if one pair split, the whole damned thing would fall apart. Maggie says:

'Eventually, we had a full-on *come to Jesus* moment and asked each other, *Are we committed to this and if we are, what the fuck are we supposed to do?* There is no reason, I believe, in staying in a relationship that is full of hardship. There were so many hurt feelings that we didn't want to deal with.'

Janie's synopsis is similar: 'I was trying to communicate, but I didn't know how . . . Growing up, I wasn't really allowed to have feelings – women were expected to be these perfect people that just supported the men and were happy all the time so others would want to convert to Christianity. So, when I felt bad [with or about Maggie] I stopped communicating, and I think Maggie did too. Cody would come in between and try to help us communicate, and eventually, he said, "You guys have to sort this out."'

Janie and Maggie sought help, in the form of a couples' therapist. Such is the entrenched stigma around polyamory that they couldn't find a local professional to take the three of them, but they did find someone who was non-judgemental enough to see the two women in full knowledge and appreciation of their triad. For three months they met regularly with this therapist and told the truth to each other. They said stuff they had never said before, things that had been withheld out of fear of hurting the other person (but that actually hurt everyone anyway). This helped them, much to Cody's relief too, and they vowed to communicate more honestly and effectively with one another. They now spoke the same language, just in different dialects. This didn't happen overnight, and it wasn't easy, but two years on, not only is the unit still going strong, but Janie and Maggie get on better than ever. Yes, they still get annoyed with each other. Yes, they still say stupid things. But they apologise quickly.

Getting through such a big crisis in the first year of all living together has set this throuple up with a fairly realistic view of what long-term love looks like. It's challenge *and* joy; it's graft *and* understanding. As with Rebecca and Andy's story, what comes across is not just that communication is important, but also that understanding the *how* and *why* we communicate is key. Being curious about your loved one's history and mindscape is important. Leaving assumptions unchecked can do damage.

Janie acknowledges that her usual strategy is to bottle things up and then let them explode all over the place: 'I just get super-emotional in the moment and have to take time to process things. So, I decided to also go to therapy on my own. I learned how to journal – so whenever I was feeling anything I had to journal, asking, *What happened? How did it make me feel? Was it the person doing it or was it me perceiving them as doing something? What does this say and what am I willing to accept?*'

Therapy was just one in a long line of conscious choices that Janie has made in the last few years, each of which has been transformative.

'I didn't have the ability to make choices for myself, growing up religious, so it was really empowering to start choosing things in full awareness. I remember consciously choosing to follow my desire to have sex with women, even though it was scary. Then, after realising that I wanted to be in a relationship with both Maggie and Cody together, I remember actively choosing that – polyamory. Then, when Maggie and I were having our issues, I recall making another very conscious choice to try to learn to do things differently.'

But after one choice comes another. Just as nature never remains static, nor do humans, and there are always ramifications to each and every choice we make, some of which we can't foresee. Having chosen to be more real with one another, the throuple had all uncovered some missing pieces: things they needed for self-fulfilment that they could not find exclusively with one another. It was time, they decided, to open up. After three years of sexual fidelity, they were now each free to date and have sex with people outside of the triad. It just made sense.

Cody explains: 'We were so young. At that age, it isn't possible to state you've found the one person for the rest of your life! She wasn't the same person then as she is now and she won't be the same when she's forty, nor will any of us. So giving the additional levels of freedom in the relationship to help it grow will give us a better chance of lasting.'

Maggie agrees: 'I don't think there is anyone in a monogamous relationship who can genuinely say that their partner fulfils everything that they need. It's not so different when you have two relationships! Things are still missing sometimes – course they are – though people are often shocked to hear that.'

Cody continues: 'We know so many people who have gone through divorce, and that's the last thing we want to happen. We were open to the fact that we might have romantic feelings for someone else and want sex with someone else. We've never been people for whom sex has defined the relationship. Sure, it's one part, but really our relationship is about who we want to go home with, build our lives with. We try to focus on why we want to be together, and what our relationship offers us. The rest is just detail.'

Since opening up, Maggie has dated a couple of other men – nothing beyond 'friends with benefits' – and Cody has dated a few women. Janie dates both. At the beginning they made rules to try to help each of them feel secure – things like 1) anyone has veto power over who one person goes on a date with and 2) nobody can see someone multiple times and 3) safe sex is crucial. In the end, only the third rule has stuck.

Conversely, other rules emerged as they went along. Cody, for example, asked not to see what popped up on Janie's phone as it lay on the side table – he realised through trial and error that he didn't want to accidentally glimpse notifications from her other people. They've developed a system too, one which seems to offset any lasting issues by tackling them before and during the problem itself. Usually, the three of them will have a starter conversation first, just to make sure everyone is comfortable with whatever connection is being proposed. Then, when whatever it is has taken place, the throuple return to the kitchen table and have another talk. This is rarely about sharing lots of details about what actually happened – nobody bothers to relate who kissed who where and how many items of clothing were present – but about offering an important space for everyone to bring up any difficult feelings and (hopefully) be reassured.

Another practical step the triad took was to ensure that each aspect of the relationship gets enough attention, but also that each individual can have their space. What this looks like is as follows:

- There are always four date nights inked in the diary per month. These include one for each side of this relationship triangle (Cody and Maggie/Maggie and Janie/Janie and Cody) and one for the triangle itself.
- There is also effort made to lovingly offer one another time with a specific member of the triad, if that is what's required. Maggie might say, *I've not spent much time with Janie lately, Cody – do you mind doing your own thing tonight?* and he's cool with that. Or maybe Maggie will say, *Cody, Janie and I have been snagging a bit again, so we're going to head out together for drinks on Saturday and have some fun.*
- Time alone is valued. *I really need to zone out tonight,* Janie might say to both her lovers. *I'm disappearing into my room for an evening, okay?* And yes, it is okay. Not just okay, but respected.

Is this an overly clinical way to approach relationships? It's certainly pragmatic, but what's wrong with that? Most relationships don't include anything like this kind of formalised appraisal, and having 'space' is often more a punishment or rejection than a responsible and adult act of self-care. I know that, even five years ago, I would have looked at this kind of 'relationship meeting' and dismissed it as weird or even boring. These days I disagree with my younger self wholeheartedly. Why shouldn't we plan and care for the upkeep of our relationships as we might our beautiful home? Why shouldn't we check in with a monthly or bi-annual appraisal? Is it so bad to examine satisfaction levels? To regularly assess if we're aligned? It means we no longer have to throw something/someone away the minute it hurts; by keeping comms open at all times, we can avoid nasty resentments and get back on the right track more quickly. Few of us relish having tough conversations – it's hardly easy to be upfront and say, *When you did this I felt X and Y because of A and B* – but it is crucial for maintaining intimacy. So why not carve out time for that?

If you know you are entering a period of change (or even if you're not), then making sure you designate a sacrosanct window of time to bringing stuff up could be a valuable and respectful move. Also, it allows the rest of your time together to be more free-flowing and romantic. The first time Maggie had sex with another man, the throuple's pre-established communication process was, for Cody at least, heaven-sent. He had been feeling jealous, believing that Maggie was losing interest. Once he had uttered his fears out loud, and Maggie was able to reassure him that she loved him more than ever and had no intention of going anywhere, things transformed. Cody felt secure and closer to her than before. Reflecting on his feelings, he had assumed that *if Maggie has sex with another man, she no longer wants me*, based on his only experience of a partner having sex with another man while still in a relationship with him. That was back in high school when his girlfriend had cheated on him with another guy, whom she then left him for. Cody had superimposed his past trauma onto the present. But this was *not* the same scenario at all. Once he understood that, he relaxed. By taking a risk and communicating about what he was feeling, he gave himself permission to have a new experience of a similar situation. A better one. A healing one.

Having gone through changes and learnt so much, what advice does Cody have for anyone considering being part of a committed throuple?

'Don't treat it the same as a couple [because] we had our biggest problems when we were trying to make a two-person relationship work with a third. I had to accept that there would be weeks where I would see more of one person than the other. Once we stopped trying to make everything equal and rolled with it more, it was all much more enjoyable. This kind of relationship doesn't work for everyone – maybe not most people actually. It's just that I want people to know that it *can* work.'

Choice and Communication – In Essence

Communication is so much more than just words to express how you are feeling or what you are thinking. Learning how to communicate more confidently and authentically can have a profoundly positive impact on your relationships. Constructive communication is not an insurance policy against conflict, but a tool that enables you to minimise destructive arguments and be better understood. It can turn conflict into closeness. No longer is someone your 'partner in crime' but your 'partner in *conflict*'.

Choice and Communication – Inquiry

Your communication blueprint – an investigation

As always, I am going to ask you now to think back. How did you learn to communicate? What are your rules or your assumptions about what constitutes communication – how you *should* or *shouldn't* communicate, and how you believe others should do so too? Investigating how you express yourself can be a multi-stage project, a bit like an archaeological dig. First, you need to identify the massive boulders and remove the blocks. Only then can you use a small brush to dust off the dirt. *Now* you can see the finer details of your blueprint, the intricacies of your communication. In keeping with this, let's start with a general inquiry, keeping a broad view on your communication style, before focusing on the details. We'll then follow up with a couple of practical exercises.

1. Do you usually communicate what you are thinking and feeling, or do you tend to hide it? It might take some time to figure this out, particularly if you have been self-censoring for years so that it's become almost automatic. Think about something relatively mild you felt in response to another's actions. Next to it, write down your

reaction; what you did and why and, if relevant, how that left you feeling. It's important not to judge or self-censor here, just to be honest and curious. Here's an example:

What happened*: A friend texts to cancel at the last minute. I say it's fine.*

My reaction: *I say it's fine because I don't want to look clingy. I feel like I should be nice and say it's okay, but actually, I feel mucked around. The resentment lingers all day.*

2. None of us is a perfect communicator all the time, and we all have favourite underhand ways of expressing ourselves. Think of what tactics you resort to when you're upset. Mine are sarcasm, snide comments and passive aggression. I also love just seething quietly in the corner. It's good to know your go-to poor communication methods.

3. How does your family communicate? Do any of your answers to Question 2 sound familiar? (Mine certainly do.)

4. When was the last time you communicated something important to someone and it worked? You really felt like they heard you. How did that feel? Did that relationship change afterwards? If so, was there some emotional risk? And when did trying this go wrong? How did they react – did they cut you off, get defensive, problem solve instead of just listening? How did that make you feel?

5. Who, in your life, gets to see the *real* you? And why them? If nobody, then why not? Your answers will hopefully indicate what you need to make that 'safe container' (see page 187) for constructive communication happen.

6. Now it's time to zoom in on your body when intense emotions come up. Do you know the sensory ways your emotions show up? Make a

list of feelings and their accompanying sensation. It's easy to think of emotions as just turning up, but they have a physical element too. Where do you think 'shaking' with anger comes from? So, ask yourself about the other emotions. Create your personal inventory of sensations and feelings to discover the best ways to discharge those sensations before you communicate constructively. Between you and me, I know my jaw locks when I'm angry and lifting heavy weights helps release some tension.

Now What?

Hopefully you've now got some clearer ideas on your communication profile. You might feel angry or miffed after discovering the origin of your communication flaws, i.e. the deconstructive communication patterns you observed growing up. That's normal and allowed – when we learn a healthier way to do things, there is often a period when we feel short-changed by the fact that we weren't taught it earlier. But remember, your caregivers were (almost always) trying to do the best they could with what they were given themselves. Try to focus on your gratitude for your new blueprint, rather than on your aggravation at the original one.

Do congratulate yourself on all the small, positive changes. Don't expect yourself to change in the most linear, consistent way. Instead, allow for some regression in your communication style, particularly if you're under a lot of stress. Remember how for Janie and Maggie it was hit and miss at the beginning when they first started to consciously try to communicate more clearly with one another? That's normal and even healthy. The only thing that really needs to be consistent is your desire to just keep going. Expect to need to be forgiven. And be ready to forgive others too.

CHAPTER TEN

CHOICE AND CHANGE

Happier Even After – *Anita's Story (iii)*

'You can't help your own feelings. You can only help how you react to them. Disappointing or hurting people is probably inevitable, but going forward in my relationships I don't want to leave things unsaid out of fear.'

Remember Anita and her boyfriend Andrea, from Chapter One? How one couple could navigate so much was inspiring. They showed me how conscious non-monogamy could work and I was awestruck at their openness.

Imagine my surprise, then, when I discovered that they had separated. Six years after they met, and one year after our first interview, Anita and Andrea decided to stop being a couple. When I heard this news, I was shocked. I even thought about ignoring it, worried about what my reader might think and how their faith in choice might be lessened if I said *and then they just broke up*. But I also knew that to omit this very important part of their story was to go against all this book is really about.

Why was I looking for that happy-ever-after ending anyway? That was some serious unconscious bullshit on my part. Wasn't fulfilment and growth the real measure of success? Who was to say that Anita and

Andrea might not be more fulfilled and happier now, apart? I had to practise what I preach.

I stopped wishing for reconciliation and became curious about context instead. What had changed between them, I asked Anita? And how did it and what had they learnt?

'It had stopped feeling good. I didn't feel seen, listened to. I think we were both a bit stuck, relating to each other in the same ways, and the communication broke down. Neither was giving the other what they needed, and so we were just causing harm to each other.'

Saddened by the mess and tired from constant conflict, Anita and Andrea recognised a stalemate. They were still Anita and Andrea, but no longer Anita *and* Andrea. That old relationship was gone. Could they build a new one? Quite possibly. But they had to completely let go of the past if that was ever going to happen.

It wasn't so much about admitting defeat as admitting change. They decided to take at least two months with almost no contact at all. Anita spent this time grieving something specific: the fact that this relationship hadn't become the perfect dream connection she thought it would. She had to mourn the idea that Andrea would always 'get' her, and that she would 'get' him back. There was also a big Andrea-and-Anita-shaped hollow in her life and, having previously communicated several times a day, the silence was now deafening.

'There comes a point where something has to break completely so it can be fixed. I don't mean fixed as in glued together in the same shape as before but fixed as in re-modelled: same pieces, different shape. It was like we were a vase. I had begun to look at the vase and think maybe I didn't like it any more. So, I resented it and even tried to crack it a few times but then put it back on the shelf. Eventually I smashed the vase, once and for all. Now it was really broken and could never be a vase again. But it could be made into a beautiful bowl, maybe. Something not new but totally different.'

After ten weeks apart, Anita and Andrea met up again for a long walk. The familiarity was beautiful but also not absolute. For a couple of months, they rekindled. Their attraction, which had dwindled massively in the preceding months, had resurfaced. They decided to dump labels and just be an important person in each other's lives. In this way they deliberately recreated who they were, focusing more on the good stuff, the energy and activities they love sharing and what they love to do together. They began to meet every two weeks to go for dinner, have sex, watch a film or hang out with Anita's children. They stopped sending each other messages throughout the day and just spoke on the phone every few days instead. Most of all they gave one another permission to put themselves first and to trust that, now they were both being consistently honest, whatever happened would be just right.

'I'm not in love with him right now,' Anita told me at the time: 'But I wouldn't rule out us falling for each other again in the future. If that happened, though, it would be a new relationship. I think so much of the hurt and pain I felt was about the shattering of the illusion and about grieving the expectations around him or any relationship. I had to let go of all those entrenched ideas so that I could love him and care about him now as a person who has his own needs and feelings and not someone who could always continue to make me feel good. Because when somebody makes us feel good, we want them to do that forever. Thinking they can do that? *That's* the real illusion.'

Seven months on from the break, Anita and Andrea have agreed on their new framework. It includes hugs, a call when needed and a physical meet-up every few weeks. This is not just to ease the transition into something new, but also because they still care deeply for one another. Is this what a conscious ending looks like? Each one is different, of course; there are no specific rules for an ending to be conscious other than that it is explicitly stated between the parties involved. Ideally, it will also be done in a respectful way, with an agreement for how to move forward with as much positivity as possible. But what does that Rolling Stones song say? *You can't always get what you want*. Sometimes there's just too much hurt or misunderstanding to allow for the kind of constructive communication required to co-create a satisfying and/or compassionate ending.

How do we get to this more compassionate place? I suspect it is easier to achieve a conscious ending if we have begun more consciously. I now see what a gift this latest segment in Anita's story is. Their relationship offers a demonstration of how to start *and end* something consciously. By consciously, I don't mean cleanly. Quite the opposite, in fact: these two freely concede to having just as much shit to deal with as the next person. This, too, is a gift because it means we can't afford them any special kind of status. They are self-educated people who choose to love the way that feels most meaningful to them. Just because they are working hard on self-awareness doesn't mean they don't feel anger or say nasty things when hurt or under emotional pressure. The difference is that they choose to come back and look again, apologise and repair. *What's going on here for me?* they ask themselves. *How can I be true to myself without destroying someone else?*

For Anita and Andrea, the answer was to split. Just as theirs was not the average union, it was also not a particularly normal separation either.

'It's not an "ending" with sharp edges, but more like an "ebbing" – the decision to let the tide go out on our relationship. We tried to let the wave go out just a little bit, but that didn't feel right for long either. So now we need to let it go all the way out and leave the shoreline clear. Getting to this decision was neither a neat nor linear process. We've been navigating our latest shift towards a romantic separation for more than six months. We've shouted and cried. We've grieved and rebuilt, and then grieved again. All we can do is trust the wisdom of our feelings and body and find the courage to speak that truth to one another.'

Anita is now single for the first time in twenty years, and she is also very happy with her choice. My secret desire for them to stay together and 'make it through' highlighted to me how strong my own underlying blueprint still is. With slight detachment and less of an appetite for any one specific outcome, we can notice better the potential in these losses

– how Anita's 'hollow' left space for newness; how endings lead to new beginnings. Love – conscious love, at least – is as much about space as it is about togetherness. It is as much about knowing when and how to deconstruct something as it is about understanding how to construct it. Maybe it is during the times of change, as a relationship moves from one state to another, that we can see most clearly. It's true that first impressions matter, but what about last impressions? You wouldn't write a story without an ending. Or watch a film intending to leave it twenty minutes before the credits. Every relationship is, in many ways, a story, and memorable stories need a strong conclusion. Just because you have an ending, doesn't mean you can't then have a sequel with that same person. Or a whole new story with someone else. But the ending itself will set the tone for what comes after. And it will honour what's come before.

Coping with Change

Everything you've learnt in this book can help you deal with and lean into change in relationships. Change, after all, is a central tenet of choice, since we can't make choices without being open to change. The other thing is that change is unavoidable – something the natural world around us knows and demonstrates very well. As the Buddhist theory of impermanence goes: *change is the* only *constant thing in life, that which exists across all lives, regardless of circumstance or geography.*

Nobody can guarantee where they will be and how they'll feel in three or five years' time, and this applies to all our relationships. Focus changes. Goals move. We go through personal triumphs and crises that fundamentally edit who we are and, often, who we love.

However much we might develop as people, we are still fallible. So the only question is, *how to respond?* Will you surrender to, or fight against, change? We know nothing lasts forever, so the sooner we abandon 'forever' as the summit, the better.

What, then, can we do to prepare for it? How can we come through big changes intact, particularly those we did not consciously choose? What about the times when life throws us a curveball, and we feel disempowered? How can we grieve without disappearing? The acronym below outlines my main suggestions for surviving – and even thriving – through periods of great change.

C – compassion. First and foremost, have compassion for yourself if you are going through something huge. Whether or not it seems huge to anyone else is irrelevant. Castigating yourself only increases any pain you are feeling. Speak kindly to yourself and delight in all the tiny victories. Try to catch yourself in the act of dismissing or belittling your own feelings.

H – help. Asking for help is an act of courage. Help, in the form of psychological or practical support, is what we all need when going through massive change. So don't be afraid to ask for it or accept it when it comes.

A – acceptance. Of course you're going to rail against this huge, unwanted change. Returning to a place of acceptance, however – acceptance of the things you cannot change and identification of the things you can – will help to move you forward.

N – non-judgement. Try, as much as possible, to cultivate an attitude of non-judgement and curiosity about what comes next. There is a chance it may be better, and things will make sense looking back. Hold the door open to future possibilities. Even if you can't see what's beyond it.

G – gratitude. Yes, it's hard when we're distressed to be grateful for anything. But look at what you *do* still have. Look at what you *have* achieved. What you *do* still enjoy. This isn't about being all jolly when things actually feel bleak. It's about your outlook: seeing the glass as half full.

E – externalising. Big changes bring big emotions. During particularly emotional periods of your life, it's normal to feel like an eggshell that could crack at the tiniest tap. Externalising some of these thoughts and feelings is crucial – expressing yourself and what you're going through will help you to keep processing it and moving forwards, however incrementally. Put something tangible down somewhere. Get what you are feeling *out*.

Change Your Attitude Towards Change

Have you heard the Chinese parable about the man and his horse?

There was once an old farmer who lived in a tiny village in the countryside. He was poor but had this beautiful white horse that was clearly worth a fortune. People often asked to buy the horse, but the old man refused because the horse was his friend, and who sells their *friend*? They all thought he was mad. The man continued to be poor. The horse continued to be beautiful.

One morning the farmer woke up and went to the stables to feed the horse, but his beloved friend was gone. When the farmer told the neighbours of his loss, they commiserated. 'What terrible luck,' they said. But the farmer couldn't be so sure. 'Maybe,' he replied. *Maybe.* Next day the horse returned, bringing with it three wild horses. Now the neighbours said, 'How wonderful . . . what good luck!' Again, the farmer wasn't so sure. 'Maybe,' he once again uttered. The following day the farmer's son, who was also the main worker, tried to ride one of the wild horses and broke his leg. 'Such terrible luck,' said the neighbours. 'Maybe,' the farmer repeated. The following day military officials came to draft men for the army but didn't take the farmer's son because his leg was broken. 'What good fortune!' the neighbours believed. Again, his mantra was maybe. *Maybe.*

And so the tale goes on in a similar vein. It could continue endlessly. There are a thousand different ways to tell it, but the essential message is the same: there is no good change versus bad change; there is just change + thoughts and feelings about the change.

I often bring this parable to mind during times of disappointment and frustration, as well as times of great success. Its message helps me stay grounded and reminds me that my reaction to a situation could be as powerful as any actual physical change. The story wants us to try to simply be and not to immediately judge whatever situation we're in. It's still okay to celebrate the wins and commiserate the losses, but how we view those things may change as we can't see what's around the corner. Remember that *more will be revealed;* our perspective on life events changes as circumstances unfold. There is nothing wrong with figuring out what we want, but when we are hell-bent on a destination, we try to bend everything to our will to get there. That's when we need to step back and say *maybe.*

Maybe, maybe, maybe. So much of Western thought focuses on *yes* or *no,* on *I want* or *I don't want.* We are so intent on avoiding 'bad' change and encouraging the 'good' change that we can easily become controlling. But if we change *with* our environment rather than *against* it, we stand a better chance of consciously adapting positively to our new situation.

Endings, especially, are difficult. Most difficult, perhaps, when we don't direct them, feeling instead that something has been thrust upon us – a change we didn't initiate or even want and that we haven't orchestrated. We often resort to our unconscious coping methods to defend against the unknown. One of the most conscious choices I have ever made took place in an opulent basement in Central London. It was the fourth session of couple's therapy with my wife B in a series of eight that was intended to help us learn to communicate better and get stronger. But it was also during this halfway point that I found the courage to say what I intuitively already knew, which was: *for me, this relationship is over.*

I did not mean *end of story*, but more like *this instalment is complete.* In truth, I had known it for some time but had been too scared to believe or say it. Often I wonder if there is little more to choosing change than simply deciding you want it just one grain more than you fear it. It is that last grain of sand, after all, that makes the scales tip.

I can't say B was happy about it. In many ways she wanted change too, but she also liked the status quo. *Why couldn't we live together, still, and just be different?* she asked. *Why did we need to physically separate in order to change the way we saw each other?*

These were good and valid questions, particularly given that we had both worked hard to adapt our relationship from age-old ideas about having to cohabit. If spouses could live apart and be in love, then why couldn't they live together and be just friends? I had no argument for this. I had only my heart's words, and they were *because I don't want that.* For me, what felt right was to physically as well as romantically separate. I needed to sleep in my own bed and live, either alone or with our son, in my own, individual space.

Everything we had been through together eased this transition. We'd opened up our relationship, had other lovers and had considered the Tim Burton and Helena Bonham Carter model of separate living. But what I realised at that point was that, while my wife was still committed to 'making it work as it was', I was committed to 'making it work as it could be'.

I loved this woman, and even though our romantic connection was coming to an end, we still had so much between us. Twelve whole years of the good times and the bad. A child we deeply loved and whom we didn't want to suffer in this process. Why would we throw all that away by being strangers to one another? A painful separation wasn't our destiny. Yes, there were things to work through, and yes, we needed some space in which to do that. There were things there to forgive before we could achieve a genuine friendship. But the idea that we would either hate one another or drift out of one another's lives, after all these shared experiences? That was hideous to me. We didn't need to disappear, but to transform.

Choice and Change – In Essence

Change is inevitable as time passes. Finding ways to embrace that will help you navigate the emotions that come with it. Change can appear positive or negative, but in fact, change is just . . . change. *We* prescribe its value judgement. Approaching change with emotional maturity involves **C**ompassion, **H**elp, **A**cceptance, **N**on-judgment, **G**ratitude and **E**xternalising. When unwanted change is thrust upon us, we are entitled to feel angry and upset. We may even disintegrate for a period of time, and that's okay, so long as we can keep in touch with faith – the belief that there are rich things waiting for us beyond this hopelessness.

Choice and Change – Inquiry

What would you change if you weren't scared?

What might you say, if you felt able?

If the thing that you most wanted to change about yourself, or your life, was to actually change tomorrow, how would you know? What might feel different? What has improved?

Can you think of a time when, like Cody, you have imprinted something scary that happened in the past onto a vaguely similar situation in the present? Is there anything going on now that reminds you of a dynamic you've had in the past? What would it look like to step back and consider that it might not go the way it's always gone? Can you give yourself permission to have a new experience? What would that look like?

Think about times in the past when you have been subject to an unwanted change that made no sense to you at the time, but that you later appreciated. Something you were sure was 'bad' before your perspective changed. Write down how you felt about it and how you look at the whole situation now. Look at what you've written. Can knowing that things go in strange and unexpected directions help you to face a current challenge or change with a bit more faith?

Now What?

Ideally, this inquiry has sparked some insight and loosened up your mind a little to change. Maybe you've identified some key areas of your life that you would really like to change – things you haven't addressed out of fear or self-doubt. If you've had an a-ha moment, you might be itching to get on with it. My advice is to go gently from here. Conscious changes involve doing things with responsibility and commitment, which means you rush them at your peril. *One step at a time.* Or, as E.L. Doctorow said about writing a novel – though this absolutely applies to any big project – 'It's like driving a car at night. You can only see as far as your headlights, but you can make the whole trip that way.'

EPILOGUE – THE SPIRIT OF CHOICE

When I first began to mull over this book, pulling together all my personal and professional experience of why and how we have relationships with one another, I had one message to get across*: we must be true to ourselves or else this life is just a farce.* Whatever your yearnings in matters of sex and love, you should be allowed, if you wish, to fulfil them, provided you don't deliberately trample over others to get your desires met. The way I had intended to get this message across was via a book focused on all the different iterations of conscious non-monogamy (by then, I had spent some time in the world of CNM and met some interesting people with non-conformist ideas), spreading the word about the viable 'other' relationship structures that are often disrespected or misunderstood.

By the time I sat down to write this book, however, I no longer believed that focusing solely on CNM was the answer. There was something broader, bigger, that I felt more passionately about, which encompassed monogamy *and* conscious non-monogamy, and plenty of other ways of being as well. And if there's one thing I know about writing a book, it's that you need to feel passionate about your subject if you are going to reach the end. I had to ask myself: what was the one big thing I had learnt in the last decade of my life – the decade when I had been sober, in and out of therapy and on a 'path' to some kind of vague enlightenment – that I could no longer live without?

Autonomy was the answer. The ability to tune into all parts of my being and make decisions based on my truth. And this didn't seem possible without first recognising and cultivating choice. How can we ever become mentally or emotionally agile enough to entertain new ways of being if we don't even know they are there? I wanted to tell stories about choice. Not just about making one life-changing choice (like the choice to become polyamorous, for example, in Alex's story; Chapter 2), but also about making successive choices (the choice to be non-monogamous, polyamorous, celibate and then monogamous, as in Cath's story; Chapter 8) or the choice to think quite differently (Hannah's story; Chapter 2); the choice to encourage others to think differently (Vix's story; Chapter 7) and to begin *and* end differently (Anita's story; Chapter 1). I wanted to explore how someone might finally make the choice to walk away from horrifying abuse (Dominic's story; Chapter 7); to address some things that keep human beings stuck, sometimes for years, in coercive, co-dependent dynamics (Cassie's story; Chapter 5); to discover how choice means expansion and builds resilience (Cody, Maggie and Janie's, and Rebecca's stories both in Chapter 9).

I felt sure that telling other people's stories, interspersed with therapeutic reflections and inquiries, would be helpful for readers interested in opening things up, whether that be their marriages or just their minds. What I couldn't know when I started writing *Love* and *Choice*, however, was just how helpful other people's stories would be to me. I did not fully appreciate how much the honesty and courage of those I interviewed would add to my own life as it progressed alongside the writing of this book. I was so grateful for the tales I had been told, their reality and wisdom, as I traversed my way along the rocky path of love, going through two major relationship break-ups within one year.

Amicable and imperfect, the separation with B, my civil partner, was a conscious ending of sorts as we worked towards reshaping our family unit and becoming friends after twelve years as lovers. I realised I no longer wished to be polyamorous and wanted to focus my romantic energy purely in one direction: in my existing relationship with A. We (A and I) dreamt of creating a life-story together, building a committed relationship that involved, when desirable, the occasional foray into conscious non-monogamy. But our passion was stronger than our foundations, and this meant that our relationship didn't survive the challenges we faced. It was here that I learnt a vital lesson: love alone is not enough. Things went from messy to unmanageable. It did not matter that I was working as a therapist, nor that I was also writing a book about relationships. Despite knowing that we were getting it wrong, I couldn't find the way to make it right. As the year progressed, this relationship continued until, one day, we shattered again and it was, very suddenly, impossible. All the breaks meant we'd lost some crucial pieces along the way. What followed was a slow and confusing separation that hurt like hell. It hurt. Like hell.

With hindsight, I now suspect that this relationship ended as it did because of the way it had begun. The brutal irony is that sometimes the life lessons we learn within a specific relationship are exactly those which, once learnt, might have allowed that relationship to survive. We try to honour our previous relationships by doing better next time with someone else. My fallout from that four-year-long union was enormous. Left with so many unanswered questions and in full knowledge of the ways in which I had screwed up, I questioned both my ability to write this book and my ability to have a conscious relationship with anyone. It turned out that, with enough time and the right kind of external support, my heart recovered. Not completely, but the hurt was no longer paralysing.

Did I make choices in my previous relationships? Yes. Were they conscious? Sometimes. Did I have a choice over the unconscious choices I made? Not really. Am I making more conscious choices now than in my past? Yes. And when I make conscious choices now, do I always know where they will take me? Of course not! To make a choice is to take a turn not knowing exactly what's up ahead. *Put in the action and let go of the consequence,* as goes the excellent epithet from Alcoholics Anonymous, the twelve-step fellowship of which I'm proud to be a member. Sometimes we are best off making the next right choice and then *trusting something* – the universe/a higher force or power/any energy more substantial than ourselves – that what comes next is what we need. It is this spiritual perspective, this conscious decision-making combined with trust, that allows me to make difficult decisions knowing I can't control them. I hope you have your way too.

It is quite something, I have discovered, to write a therapeutic book promoting romantic love and conscious choice while simultaneously having one's own belief in both of those things completely shaken. Yet it is also fitting, I think, since trials and tribulations are universal, no matter who you are. We are all on a creative journey towards self-awareness. I wish you luck on yours as I continue mine.

SUGGESTED FURTHER READING

This is certainly not a list of every seminal book written about the topics covered here. There is a wealth of other material, and more is being published on the world of relationships and conscious non-monogamy with each passing year. These are some of the books that have influenced me and inspired my writing.

Barker, M-J, *Rewriting the Rules: An Anti Self-help Guide to Love, Sex and Relationships* (Routledge, 2018)

Beattie, Melody, *Codependent No More: How to Stop Controlling Others and Start Caring for Yourself* (Hazelden FIRM, 2018)

Brown, Brené, *Daring Greatly: How the Courage to Be Vulnerable Transforms the Way We Live, Love, Parent and Lead* (Avery Publishing Group, 2015)

Chödrön, Pema, *The Places That Scare You: A Guide to Fearlessness* (HarperNonFiction, 2004)

Easton, Dossie and Hardy, Janet, *The Ethical Slut: A Practical Guide to Polyamory, Open Relationships and Other Freedoms in Sex and Love* (Ten Speed Press, 2017)

Fern, Jessica, *Polysecure: Attachment, Trauma and Consensual Nonmonogamy* (Thorntree Press, 2020)

Gahran, Amy, *Stepping off the Relationship Escalator: Uncommon Love and Life* (Off the Escalator Enterprises, 2017)

Gendlin, Eugene, *Focusing: How to Gain Direct Access to Your Body's Knowledge* (Rider, 2003)

LePera, Dr Nicole, *How to Do the Work: Recognise Your Patterns, Heal from Your Past and Create Your Self* (Orion Spring 2021)

Levine, Peter, *Waking the Tiger: Healing Trauma* (North Atlantic Books, 1997)

Levine, Amir and Heller, Rachel, *Attached: Are You Anxious, Avoidant or Secure? How the Science of Adult Attachment Can Help You Find – and Keep – Love* (Bluebird, 2019)

Lunn, Natasha, *Conversations on Love* (Viking, 2021)

Maté, Gabor, *In the Realm of Hungry Ghosts: Close Encounters with Addiction* (North Atlantic Books, 2011)

Maté, Gabor, *When the Body Says No: The Cost of Hidden Stress* (Vermilion, 2019)

Perel, Esther, *Mating in Captivity: How to Keep Desire and Passion Alive in Long-term Relationships* (Hodder & Stoughton, 2007)

Perel, Esther, *The State of Affairs: Rethinking Infidelity* (Harper, 2017)

Poole Heller, Diane, *The Power of Attachment: How to Create Deep and Lasting Intimate Relationships* (Sounds True Inc., 2019)

Richo, David, *How to Be an Adult in Relationships: The Five Keys to Mindful Loving* (Shambhala Publications Inc., 2002)

Richo, David, *Triggers: How We Can Stop Reacting and Start Healing* (Shambhala Publications Inc., 2019)

Saltman, Bethany, *Strange Situation: A Mother's Journey into the Science of Attachment* (Scribe, 2020)

Taormino, Tristan, *Opening Up: A Guide to Creating and Sustaining Open Relationships* (Cleis Press, 2008)

Van der Kolk, Bessel, *The Body Keeps the Score: Brain, Mind and Body in the Healing of Trauma* (Penguin Random House, 2015)

Veaux, Franklin and Rickert, Eve, *More Than Two: A Practical Guide to Ethical Polyamory* (Thorntree Press, 2014)

Welwood, John, *Journey of the Heart: The Path of Conscious Love* (HarperCollins, 1998)

Wilby, Rosie, *Is Monogamy Dead?: Rethinking Relationships in the 21st Century* (Accent Press, 2017)

Wilby, Rosie, *The Breakup Monologues: The Unexpected Joy of Heart-break* (Green Tree, 2021)

ACKNOWLEDGEMENTS

It is impossible to thank everyone who has influenced me creatively or helped me to arrive at the writing of *Love and Choice*. There are some, however (both people and places), who have played an obvious part. These include:

The London Library in St James's Square, a place that holds great significance for me in my professional and creative life. I am so happy that I get to work in such a beautiful, peaceful space.

CCPE (Centre for Counselling and Psychotherapy Education), the transpersonal psychotherapy hub in Little Venice where I have learnt many of the therapeutic ideas that are contained within this book, and a great deal about myself.

Thank you so much to Carole, for being a safe emotional harbour. You inspire gratitude and faith.

I am so grateful to those in the publishing world who helped this book come to fruition. These include the team at RML, especially my fabulous literary agent, Rachel Mills. I feel very lucky to have you in my corner. Without that conversation with you, back in early 2020, I would never have run into the idea for this book.

Thank you to the team at Hodder Studio. To Harriet Poland, for confidently pressing *Love* and *Choice* forward with purpose and precision. To Kwaku Osei-Afrifa, whose beady editorial eyes and wise counsel were second only to their effervescent commentary at various stages during the writing process.

I am also grateful to those experts or researchers who were happy to share their knowledge with me: Meg-John Barker, Dr Lori Bisbey and Helen Fisher. Thank you to all the writers quoted in this book as well as all those experts and creatives (too many to namecheck here) who have influenced my ideas with their work.

I am indebted to *all* the open-hearted people who spoke to me about their choices. Your honesty helped me to remain non-judgemental and curious – to shape my thoughts about love, relationships and conscious communication. Thank you to everyone whose brains and hearts I picked over dinner or at the pub or who helped to contextualise stories that were then told from the perspective of another – Andrea and Andy. Thank you to Alison F., Leng, Caleb and Bella Rose. Most particularly, thank you to those who engaged in a much fuller interview process, and whose stories run through this book: Alex*, Anita, Cassie*, Cath*, Cody, Dominic*, Dmitri*, Elaine, Hannah, Janie, Jon*, Maggie, Sandy* and Vix.

I am grateful to those who read and offered feedback on early drafts or certain chapters as I went along, including Helen and Julia, and thank you to Toby for providing emergency printing services!

Thank you to Ali, for your encouragement and brainpower during the early stages of this project. The endless conversations we had about love and relationships, as well as our lived experienced, provided much inspiration for this book.

Thank you to Bella, who read each new chapter as it arrived and who has been unrelentingly supportive of my writing for almost fifteen years. Your ongoing friendship means the world to me.

Thank you so much to Carole, for being a safe emotional harbour. You inspire gratitude and faith.

I owe a great deal to the everyday backing of my closest friends – you know who you are – whose humour and compassion, though not always explicitly related to my writing, enables me to tackle life as a sensitive soul with enormous emotions. Thank you especially to Jenny Glithero – your help with Chapters Five and Six is particularly appreciated. Also, not many people can make me snort with laughter from their hospital bed. Your courage and resilience are inspirational.

Thank you to Cecile, for your beauty, kindness, humour and understanding. For turning up when I was broken and allowing me, quite simply, to be myself. You have taught me that love need not equal sacrifice. It is a life-changing lesson. I am so grateful to have learnt it.

Thank you, most of all, to my son, Rufus. If there is one thing I want for you, as your mama, it is for you to be able to access and make nourishing choices for yourself as you age, pulling towards you all that brings love and fulfilment and letting go of that which makes you smaller in any way. May you always be creative and curious. You are the greatest gift of all.

ABOUT THE AUTHOR

Lucy Fry is a writer and speaker. She is author of a memoir, *Easier Ways to Say I Love You* (Myriad Editions, 2020), and a narrative non-fiction book, *Run, Ride, Sink or Swim: A Rookie's Guide to Triathlon* (Faber & Faber, 2015). Lucy is a freelance journalist and former wellbeing columnist for the *Sunday Telegraph*. She has written hundreds of articles for broadsheets, magazines and websites and is a regular radio and podcast guest.

Lucy is also a psychotherapist. She received training at the Centre for Counselling and Psychotherapy Education in West London and the Institute for Arts in Therapy and Education.

She lives in South London with her son. You can reach her on Instagram @lucy_fry_writer or on Twitter @lucycfry. Also, see her website: www.lucyfry.co.uk.